My days are lonely and
Disturbing
Wretched

I am stressed
Crying now; night and day

My life isn't easy
I think I am being punished for something, but
what I truly do not know.
Why does life have to be so hard and confusing?

Why do I have to be born to feel such pain and
anguish?

What have I done that is so vile that I cannot
truly get ahead in life?

What grave sin have I committed that I feel
cursed; doomed?

Why is life this unfair to me?

Ah yes the nightmares of living in sin.
Nightmares of living in a wretched world filled
with sin and evil.

What am I doing here?
Why can't I find a clean place where I can be all
alone?

Alone and away from my children that do not listen.

Away from my stresses and heartache.

Away from it all.

I need to escape but to where is the issue?
I want to run, run far away where no one can reach me; call me, email or even text me.

Escape, I need escape from this wretched life.
I need escape from it all, including Good God and Allelujah himself.

Tears, tears they are coming.
They came and went but my sorrows are still there.

Rescue me I cry but even the God above do not hear my cries; plea.

My heart fails me, I am left alone.
Left for dead until my new awakening.

Michelle
June 04, 2015

I need this to be my day where I do what I want, when I want and how I want. But truth be told, this could never ever be.

I need a life of my own
One that is stress and horror free

Confusion, confusion
Oh yes it's in me

How can I keep hope alive when hope has and have left me?

How could I have prevented this; this fall?

What do I do now that I am lost in the shuffle?
Feel like a failure
Feel like my world is closing in

Ignorance is there, but ignorance is for the weak hearted. Strength is what I need and must have.

Strength to go on despite the adversity
Heartache and pain

The will is there but the mind is oh so weak.

Michelle
June 04, 2015

On this day I ask myself and God, Good God why was I born?

Why was I made to suffer, feel so much anguish and pain?

Why am I here on this earth if life fails me?
Why put your children through this torment and anguish; hurt; pain?

What is the purpose of life, if life fails you?
Angers you to the point where you truly do not care?

What is the point of life if hope is fading?
Never lasts

What is the significance of life when I feel lost?
Feel abandoned by the one I truly love.

Is this true love or is it vexation of spirit?
What is true love if you end up feeling pain?
What is true love when the one you truly and unconditionally love with all your truth cannot save you from all the ills and pain that come your way?

What is the purpose of truly loving him when you feel lost and confused?

Questions, questions all these I have.

The pain is real
The hurt is real
Too much agony

I am but alone in a house
His home

I am the only one there in this home
World

Am I but his shadow?

No I cannot be. Spirits and or energy do not cast
a shadow; they are just there in the light; dark.

There are different lights you know, but what of
this beautiful greyish light?

What do I make of it and why am I sitting alone?

Michelle
June 04, 2015

Why do I feel like a fallen angel?
Why do I feel abandoned and discouraged?
Why do I feel as if all hope is gone?
Why do I feel so all alone?

My life is real but can one person go through so
much turmoil without snapping; go insane?

What is the purpose of life if you have to feel so
much hardship as well as be alone?

Wow, what a world.
What a day?
My day

Michelle Jean

I need to think and be me
Need to think and do me

I need to think
Live
Become one with something but what?

Oh yes I am confused and I truly do not know what to do.

I am waiting but it doesn't seem like God; Good God is waiting on me.

I want to run but run where?
I want to hide in the arms of someone safe and strong, but who that someone is, is a different story.

Life come and for some it goes. So why come at all if you have to meet and face hardships and pain?

Why come at all if you have to go?

Why come at all if all the world's problems cannot be solved on or in human terms?

Hope fading
Drifting
Dying

I need to become a drifter; then what would my worry be?

What would my life be like if I kept on drifting? Living from city to city, province to province without a care?

Yes I need to find me because the ME in me have and has escaped me.

I am worlds apart from Lovey and to me that's not fair. There is no escape button I could push to get to him right away. Everything takes time, years and centuries and that's a true bummer.

My way is dark right now and all I can do is write; let my emotions out as to the way I feel.

Yes problems come and they do go, but this is my way of venting, trying to keep a cool and level head.

Yes some people have alcohol and drugs, I have my writings; thoughts to you.

Hey there is no music that can help me on this day because I truly do not feel okay.

Do I want to scream and swear? Yes I do but I can't. I have to go through the cycle of life and wonder, wonder what happened for me to be this way. Yes I know this is the time of evil and death, but why can't happiness come for me?

Why can't true happiness come for you?

Why should there be so much pain here on earth?

Oh dear what a life?

I feel deserted.
Feel ashamed of the way my life is going.

I know this is temporary, but why should I feel ashamed of what is happening in my life?

Problems come and go, but only a selected few can handle them. Hence I choose to write about mine and not go ballistic and or crazy.

Life is wonderful yes, but the stress that follows isn't so great.

Michelle
June 04, 2015

Confusion sets in and I don't know where to turn. Do not know how to overcome; get over the situation I am in.

Stress comes
Staying
Can't think
Can't truly focus

I am in denial.
Don't want to accept the predicament I am in.

Confusion
Confusion

Which way do I turn?

It feels like I am losing my mind.
Feels like I am going to go insane.

Why didn't he listen?
Why didn't Lovey protect him more?

But I can't blame Lovey because he did all he could. Disobedience is a sin and when we are disobedient things happen. Things that you never thought could happen happen.

So you think where did I go wrong?
You call yourself a failure
Beat up on you

Oh what a nightmare because things are not going your way.

How do I overcome?
How do I move on?

Yes it's not so bad, but yet in my world this is bad.

In my world, not even my children take good counsel. Well not all.

Am I being punished for my behavior as a child, well teen with my mother?

Are these the consequences of my own actions?

Dear God, what have I done?

Why do I feel forsaken and discouraged?
Broken

Why am I stressing myself out so?

Yes it's not the end of the world, but in my world it might as well be.

Why can't goodness, true goodness and mercy follow me each and every day Lovey more than forever ever without end?

Why can't this truth, true goodness and mercy follow all my children each and every day Lovey more than forever ever without end?

Why can't they listen to good and true counsel?

Why can't they see the goodness that I am trying to teach and show them and accept goodness and truth forever ever without end?

Lovey, why is it so hard for me when it comes to teaching them (my children)? I need them to have good counsel as well as follow good counsel but they are truly not listening. They don't want to listen. They want to do their own thing. And when bad things happen, I beat up on myself and think I am a failure.

So why me?

Why can't I pass the buck like some mothers?

Why do I have to care so much?

Why do they (some of my children) have to cause me so much pain?

I want to escape.
Flee to somewhere where they can't find me.

I need to be on my own so that they can be on their own. They can pay their own bills; rent; buy their own food and see just how hard I had it raising them.

I need them to have responsibilities now Lovey. Hence I have to actively start looking for a place for me and only me.

Everyone is of age and to be totally truthful and honest to you Lovey; my children are pampered in many ways.

I do all for them even in my sick state hence I too am to blame in many ways.

Why did I not ask you for good and true children, children that are obedient that follow and adhere to good and true counsel?

Clean children.

Good children that would come to know you and cleave to you and your honesty and truth.

Lovey, where did I go wrong in life?

Where did I go wrong in my teachings when it comes to them?

Where did I go wrong with them?

Now I am stressed and running to you Lovey for strength in my hour of need.

My health is truly not all that great but I am trying like my mother did.

I am trying to raise them right, but in all that I've tried, I've failed.

Lovey, why my life?

Do you not see me trying?

Do you not want to help me?

I know you are keeping me alive but the pain I am going through is just too much when it comes to my children.

I truly cannot do it anymore hence I am asking you to tell me what to do.

Stop keeping closed mouth when it comes to my children. You do not keep closed mouth with me sometimes. So why are you closed mouth when it comes to my children?

Michelle

Ah Lovey it's strange how life is. This is supposed to be My Day but the mood is different in so many ways.

Lovey, let me ask you this. Humanity, well some in this world (humanity) say they praise and worship Jesus who is your son.

They also said he died on the cross for them.

Now Lovey I ask you this. Would you make your son; your only begotten son; your only child be buried amongst a murder and a thief?

Now this is your son here Lovey according to mans so called holy bible. Your only child that you had with a mortal and or human female.

This is your child that humans crucified and did all manner of evil to before he died. On top of it all, when he was on the cross in agony "they gave him vinegar to drink mingled with gall; and when he had tasted thereof, he would not drink." Matthew 27 verse 34.

Now Mark chapter 15 verses 23 gave a different account of what they gave Jesus to drink. Verse 23 says, "And they gave him to drink wine mingled with myrrh; but he received it not." Lovey this is your child that humans did this to.

THEY MURDERED THE MAN AND YOU ARE TO FORGIVE HUMANITY FOR THIS MURDER, GRAVE SIN?

Lovey, your only child got murdered by humans and you are to turn the other cheek and save humanity for murdering your only child!! You're to pretend like nothing happened!!!

HUMANITY REJECTED HIM; DID NOT ACCEPT HIM. INSTEAD THEY KILLED HIM BY CRUCIFYING HIM ON A CROSS AND YOU ARE TO FORGIVE HUMANS FOR THIS AND SAVE THEM!!

Many messengers you sent to humans to amend their dirty ways and these messengers were slaughtered; taken to the slaughter house of death and killed, and you are to be all forgiving and pretend like nothing happened?

Lovey, none stood up to Pilate and or whomever and said, this is bullshit you cannot do this. This is Lovey's child you cannot kill him.

How dare you lay a hand on him!!! He's the child of God, the God who created the heavens and the universe and you can't do this.

Not even you Lovey did anything?

Now Lovey tell me why?

You did not rain down fire and brimstone on Pilate and the wicked people of old for sacrificing your so called child to death.

You allowed the murder to take place. Now I ask you this, what type of father are you?

How much love; true love did you have for your so called son? You made him die.

You allowed his death, now I ask you this, if he was your son; pure and of you, why did you let him die?

Look at the way you are with me when I tell you I am leaving you.

Why would you allow humans to murder your only child? You are the creator of this world and universe. Humans cannot see you in your organic and or natural state. Now tell me, how are they going to see your child; son?

Now answer me this yet again, *YOU ARE THE CREATOR OF ALL LIFE AND YOU CREATED HUMANS LONG BEFORE ADAM AND EVE. WHY THE HELL WOULD YOU DIRTY YOURSELF AND LAY WITH A HUMAN BEING?*

WE PASS FILTH THROUGH OUR BODY AND YOU ARE THAT DESPARATE TO LAY WITH A HUMAN AND PROCREATE WITH HER. HAVE A SON WITH HER AND THEN HAVE HUMANS KILL HIM; CRUCIFY HIM WORSE THAN A PIG ON A CROSS BETWIXT A THIEF AND A MURDERER!!!!

WOW!!

Man you sank lower than low.

You're not even at the bottom of the barrel to the way humans depict you. Hence you made a choice to allow humans to depict you as a worthless and disgusting monster. A murderer that cares not for his child; children and people.

You sacrificed your own child to death to save wicked and evil people. Lovey, yu sick or wha?

This is your child and you jus han im ova to death jus like dat?

Yu did hate yu pickney?

Wow Lovey, this is beyond comprehension. Wicked and evil people yu gi up yu son fa?

Wicked an evil people wey nuh count yu.
Wicked an evil people wey spit pan yu and trample yu dung every chance dem get.

Wicked an evil people wey praise di Devil, Satan and Death whether male or female death.

Yu nuh naamal to regile.

Wicked and evil people Lovey?

Bumbleet yu good.
Lovey, a soh yu tan?

A soh yu weak mek yu affi gi up yu good up good up son as a sacrifice to death jus to save death's own?

Lovey fi real doah. Hence I am going to leave things as is because I more than know the true you. ___You would never sacrifice your own child to save wicked and evil people.___ _Absolutely no one can do this._ Hence the lies of man; humans have gone above and beyond anything I know.

Yes it's unfortunate that many believe this lie but this is us as humans I guess.

We readily believe lies instead of coming to you for the truth.

I know you have a voice to speak and it's unfortunate that many cannot see and know this.

I am so not here to judge; hence I will leave things alone. I know the story of Jesus is a lie hence Matthew and Mark give a different version of what happened to Jesus on the cross.

Yes I know lies are a sin and all those who wrote the story of the bible will pay and pay dearly for their lies in hell. Hence I worry about them not. What I am concerned about is the weird dreams I've been having and the toll it's taking on my health. This morning (June 12, 2015) I woke up in pain. I don't know why I am having such pain all over including these severe headaches.

Yes this is my life but why should anyone live in pain like me.

Oh well this is my life I guess and there isn't anything anyone can do about this. Hence I wrote these.

It's Friday June 12, 2015 and the pain is excruciating Lovey. I feel as if I am going to die. Yesterday I wanted to cry out for death but refrained. My body cannot take any more pain.

It cannot take any more pressure. The pain is unbearable Lovey. My body aches so much.

Are my arteries clogging up? The pressure going to the back of my head/brain is too much.

My right shoulder hurt so much that I truly don't know what to do.

My insulin burns to the point now where I feel as if I am slowly dying. I know I am allergic to insulin because I can feel the reaction. It's like when I eat too much nuts my body reacts negatively. The feel is the same with my insulin sometimes. And yes the feel is hard to describe.

Lovey I can't take this anymore hence I know why people cry out for death when they are in pain; sick.

My body cannot bare anymore man. I can't take this pain anymore. Down to the follicles of my hair hurt and this is happening more and more. I've been crying out to you about this pain and my sickness but all you've done is ignore me.

When does my aches and pain stop?

I truly can't take the pain anymore Lovey. I truly can't.

Life isn't worth going through all this pain and suffering. My head hurts more and more. I can barely go and you are not there to help me rid this pain; my suffering.

Michelle
June 12, 2015

The body is so weak Lovey
So weak

All I see around me is death.
When does death stop interfering with me?
When does death stop gnawing at my life?

Where is my strength Lovey?
Where have you gone in all of this?

Why have you abandoned me?
Why is death knocking at my door?

The pain is gone but the health is not there.
Body weak as if no life is there.

Walking is slow and sickly but I am thankful
that the pain is gone.

The house/apartment needs cleaning but I can't
manage it no more. I cannot do anything; cannot
manage the cleaning.

Bathing is becoming a struggle. I know I am
going to need something to sit on to bathe
myself real soon but I am so not worried.

My body is totally giving way. Yes I can accept
this because I know what's happening, but the
pain I cannot handle, it's too excruciating;
unbearable when it comes.

Lovey you saw my tears because I was crying and you did nothing to comfort me; ease my pain at that moment.

Lovey is this true life with you?

Is this going to be the way things are with me for the rest of my life with you?

This life; painful and hard life is not worth it. Hence I truly do not wish this on or for my worst enemy.

Why me Lovey?

Why make me feel so much pain at this stage in my life?

Why the hell should anyone feel this continuous pain when they are around you; trying to walk with you?

It's as if you are a death trap.

As if there is nothing civil about you when it comes to us.

You permit us to suffer. So it matters not what side we choose, we are damned if we do and damned if we don't literally.

Death and suffering consumes us hence she did tell me that God kills. And to be honest and truthful to you, she is not lying because all who travel your path slowly dies. We die of loneliness and suffering. So tell me, what is the difference between you and death?

You don't hear us but yet you are expecting us to care and listen to you. If people feel threatened and abandoned, feel hurt and pain they are going to want to leave. The world is full of hardship and pain, walking with you is filled with hardship and pain, who the hell want and need more suffering and pain in their life when it comes to you?

I truly don't but yet you keep me and others in situations that are not warranted. Situations that cause us hurt and pain. To top this off, you want us to praise you.

For bleeping what?

Letting sin and death including sorrow consume us and cause us true pain. Come on now man, be bleeping fair.

Just as how we are unfair to you, you are unfair to us. Hence many cannot walk on your road; turn from you and refuse you. You are too painful and it seems like you don't get it.

We choose you, but with you, the choice we make do hurt us.

Our choice is sorrowful here on earth and in all I do, plea with you, it's the same shit day after day. Happiness cannot be found with you and I've told you on numerous occasions, you truly do not make me happy. You cannot make me truly happy because happiness is not in you.

And no I will not take these words back because it's the truth. You want, but yet provide us not with places that are safe and debt free as well as death free to live in.

You cannot say you love us so and permit us to continue to suffer like this. This is not right hence I return all my pain and sufferings onto you now. Take them all because I am done, totally done with them (my pain and sufferings, health woes, financial debts and woes, family and children woes, my loneliness and your one sidedness including your loneliness and unhappiness). I need to be free hence give me back my true and good life of happiness and freedom. Give me back my financial and health riches in the physical and spiritual realm and world including the good up good up universe. Keep your anger and pain because I want no part of your depressive and unhappy world anymore. Keep your damned pain and loneliness because this is your world and not mine. I truly don't need them so keep them with you. No I do not want to do this, but I am. Death can now come to you and take your life because you are truly not fair to me and your people. You would rather let us live in sufferings and pain rather than do the right thing and help us. And don't you dare go there with the past history of my ancestors and the choice the black race made. This is Michelle you are talking to. I will not make any excuses for them because I've stopped making excuses for you. I am not them. I don't want or need to be like my ancestors, I need to be like the good and true me and you refuse to allow me to be. Hence you are my true stumbling blog and I have to bulldozer you out of my way. It's a matter of finding that bulldozer to push you infinitely and indefinitely out of my way on this day. Yes I am hurt but you cannot continue to be my stumbling block. This is truly not right come on now. You are hurting me.

You don't provide no you do, it's the pain and suffering that we have to endure that makes many walk away from you like I want to do right now.

Why Lovey?

Why abandon me like this?

Why leave me broken down like a broken down old house?

Why leave me in ruin?

If you knew you could not help me to fix me and fix the troubles and worries of your people which is our people; why ask me to write?

If you knew you cannot fix the worries and trouble of this world and or within this world and universe, why ask me to write?

Why ask me to write you a book if you were not going to be faithful and true to me and our good and true people?

My days on earth are numbered because I am feeling the pangs of death. Death wants me but I've told you, I truly do not want death to take me. You and my mother have to hold my hand so that I can walk with you both to glory in the flesh and spirit. But in all I do, you are not listening to me. Yes this morning I wrote my will again. I've told you of my good will but you are not listening. No wonder humans don't listen to you and they turn from you.

You are one sided and one way. You expect us to listen to you and do your will but yet you refuse to listen to our ailments, cries; pain.

How can we care if you as God truly do not care?

Now tell me this, what is the point of us talking and even writing to you if you truly do not listen?

Will we not feel abandoned by you?

Have I not told you I feel as if you've abandoned me?

Well what about us and our good and true will?

No, you are not just nor are you fair in many ways.

So sue me you are saying.

One day I will and let's see what you're gonna say.

Don't you dare say I can't sue you because I can and will. I will sue you for pain and suffering not just for me but for the universe, the earth, the environment, the trees, the waterways and I will definitely sue you for the pain and suffering of our good and true people both living and dead.

Don't laugh, it's just too much for me to bare. Death is too close to me again.

Just this morning (June 12, 2015) I dreamt urine in my bathroom. Dreamt mess on the toilet seat.

Lovey, I have to get my life together.

Lovey why does my life have to be so messy in the physical and spiritual realm?

Dreamt I finally had sex. So yes I lost my virginity again and I lost it to a Clarendonian. He is a singer in real life. Yes Freddie McGregor. Yes we used a condom. But Lovey, I truly do not know this man in real life; the living. Over eight (8) years of not having sex and I lost my virtue again. Wow and to a Clarendonian. Yeah me!

Damn. Goodbye Russian men, it's Clarendonian for me. But in truth though Lovey, I put no value in my dreams when it comes to me. Dreams about me are false; false hope and yes lies given to give me hope. I know dreams about me are infinite and indefinite lies hence I put absolutely no value or merit in them. They are just lies generated to keep me satisfied like I've said. This I know so I leave them alone literally.

Also dreamt this fat, well big and or stocky white man. He was about my height if not a little taller than me. And people his fat was proportioned. Even his big and fat nose. He wore a hat and I thought him to be German. I asked him if he was German but he did not answer me; he smiled. He was writing something but I could not read his writing. He was writing beside another language as if hiding his language between this language. His language was like a dot, dots. Hence he wrote between another language. Yes this is odd but then my dreams are getting odd; weird.

I don't know what happened after that but I was dancing on his leg and he asked me if I wanted him to put it in. Suffice it to say, we did not have sex. I didn't know if he was German. And no I am not being racist but if you think I am so be it. And besides I had sexual intercourse with Freddie McGregor already.

Like I said, I don't know what happened after that but like I said my bathroom had urine in it (on the floor) and it was a mess. I could not bathe. I went to get cleaning products to clean the bathroom but never returned with it. This man, same fat and or stocky white man came back. He had white legal sized paper but a bit longer and wider. He put the paper down and two crumpled up piece of yellow paper was on top of the legal paper. No writing was on the paper and the crumpled up paper or yellow paper remind me of sticky notes but crumpled. I can't remember if he was crying when he put the paper on the ground but he told me he's preparing for a funeral; burial.

Weird

But prior to this dream I dreamt I was in this place. I cannot tell you if it's Jamaica; I was just in a place. I was walking and I came across this man than looked like Peter Bunting the security minister of Jamaica. *(People I do not know if Bunting is still security minister, but he was once upon a time.)* Portia Simpson the now PM of Jamaica was sitting on a bench close to this man and when she saw me, she moved away from him and slid slowly beside this young man that looked like he was in his teens.

I don't know what happened but mi guh faass and sey sumen like yu a sit beside har? I told him she's the first illiterate to run Jamaica. She has no credentials and she never went to university.

People I went ballistic and cuss Portia. While I was cussing Portia the man wey look like Bunting got up and left and I yelled at him and said, he should run for Prime Minister.

People you all know I truly do not like this woman and if I could get her out of office and put someone that care about the people, economy and land of Jamaica into office I would.

THERE IS A HONEST AND TRUE PHYSICAL AND SPIRITUAL DISLIKE TOWARDS THIS WOMAN.

The spiritual world truly don't like her, hence Michael Manley petitions me to become Prime Minister and I keep rejecting him –think he's Satan.

People, Lovey told me to write a book twice. He never told me to become a politician. And besides Jamaica is unclean, so why would I go into unclean land that he's forbid me to go into to run for office?

Jamaica needs cleaning yes but the people must clean up self internally.

Suh Portia add your name to the list of politicians that the spiritual realm is truly against literally.

Seaga a one
Yu Portia mek two

So people as the names of the politicians come that the spiritual realm is against literally, I will let you know.

So Seaga and Portia, I truly don't want to be either of you when the spirit leaves the flesh because the both of you will have more than hell to pay in the grave literally.

An which ever man you a cozy up to in a di house of parliament, truly good luck because wey yu a hide, someone a si.

Also dreamt this. And this is weird.

Dreamt this lady – lady announcer was announcing the names of these people. ***MEN AND WOMEN OF WAR I call them.*** You could not see the lady; lady announcer. All you could see were the face of these people she was announcing. You saw their image when they were young and man they were gorgeous – beautiful, but after the war I guess they became old and not so beautiful; attractive.

The first person was male and of dark brown complexion. Nice looking. After his stint in war (fighting) he ended up on drugs. I forgot the name of the drugs he was put on and or was on. He was not on illegal drugs; he was put on medication and or was given medication to help him.

The second person was male and of the same dark brown complexion and nice looking. He had a tattoo; more like a dog tag tattoo I call it that was on his left arm; the shoulder part of his upper arm that had writing in it. In the dream I was facing him. So his mark was on the left (my left) which is his right. Around the upper part of his dog tag tattoo were clouds. Not clouds but fluffy. I just used clouds as an analogy for you to get the picture of fluffiness.

The third person was female and of dark brown complexion as well. In the dream the lady; female announcer said they killed her sister and forced her to become lesbian. Basically they made her a killing machine from what I gather. The lady announcer also said, they made her change her name. She gave the name but I cannot remember the name. Just know it was an Arabic/Muslim name that they gave her.

People I cannot remember the names of these people. I am not sure if one of their names was Ari.

Suffice it to say, I did not wait to see the fourth picture because I jumped out of my sleep.

And yes all these three people were black.

To which army they belong I could not tell you.

If I said they were American I would be lying.

This is the first time something like this has happened to me. I am being given a play by play of someone's life when they are young and old. ***Hence war; killing takes your youth and dignity from you.***

I truly cannot say anymore because this dream scared me.

Michelle
June 12, 2015

It's evening time and I am feeling a lot better.

All my pain is gone and I am more mobile. I have no appetite which is good but family what's happening to me?

My dream world is scaring me and why is this white man (crying); preparing for death?

Who is going to die?

I know my end hence I cannot prepare my children for it. I am being called home, so where ever I stop I have to because my time on earth would have come to an end.

Yes uncertainty looms because we truly do not see the afterlife. Meaning we do not know life beyond the grave.

Seen it yes, but how do I prepare you or anyone for this?

I know hell is there for all who are wicked and evil. This I know for a fact. When you get to the grave you will be judged. No not judged, but sentenced. On earth you are already judged by and or for the sins that you do. When you get to the grave you will be told and or given your number which is the time you are going to spend burning in jail; hell before your eventual death and or extinction.

One sin could have a value of 48000 years in hell.

When it comes to the lies many of you tell on Lovey, that sin weight could be infinite and indefinite burning in hell.

Yes infinite and indefinite has a time limit but infinity in my book hath no time limit; end. And yes there is such a thing as double and triple infinity for those who truly do not know.

So truly good luck to billions of you.

And don't go there. Add the amount of times you committed that one sin. Add the number of days or years.

Multiply by 48000; now calculate the rest of your sins.

Now weep.

Michelle
June 12, 2015

Well Jesus died for my sins.

Impossible!!!

One man cannot die for the sins of billions of people.

I cannot die for your sins because I did not commit them, you did. So Jesus cannot and could never die for your sins or mine.

Well Jesus is God's son and he did shed his blood to save us you are saying.

That's a strike against you right there. You've just sinned.

Did Jesus commit your sins?

No you are saying.

So how can he pay your penalty for you?

Tell me something, you said Jesus is God's son, which God?

Humans worship different gods and goddesses. Which god procreated with a human and had a human child?

Yes you can bring Greek Mythology into this.

***And Greek Myth's are just that myth's.
Stories that were made up to entertain and
fool people just like in the movies. And yes
the Greeks know the truth but yet they don't
tell the truth. Hence know the truth because
Lovey would never ever send his children on
the battlefield of death to fight him (Death)
for his and her wicked and evil own.***

Lovey would never sacrifice any of his children
to death. He over loves them too much. Yes I get
down on him but I know his truth and true love
for his good and true people.

***Life is more than valued by him, so why
would he Lovey give us good and true life
to suddenly take it away like that?***

That makes no sense.

Some of you also say Jesus is God. Now I ask
you this, ***IF GOD DIED, WHY ARE
WE STILL ALIVE?***

If Jesus was Lovey's child and he was murdered;
crucified on a cross by humans, how can Lovey
and or God save any of us? We killed his son,

thus relinquishing our right to be saved by him. Remember the law specifically said, ***"THE WAGES OF SIN IS DEATH."***

IT ALSO SAID, ***"THOU SHALT NOT KILL,"*** and humans killed his son, only begotten son as said by you and written in your holy book; bible. So if Jesus was crucified how can we be saved?

Can death save you from life or does death take your life?

Remember your so called holy book said; Jesus is the first begotten of the dead. ***So now answer me, if JESUS IS DEATH'S CHILD, THE FIRST BEGOTTEN OF THE DEAD, HOW CAN HE SAVE YOU WHEN YOU ARE THE ONE TO HAVE LIFE?***

Hence death cannot save life, death can only take life. So when we sin we die. And if you have not made amends for your sins, truly good luck in seeing Lovey because you won't. You are sinful; dirty hence your name is in death's book.

So truly woe be unto the clergies of this world because hell is truly waiting for all of them. And every arsenal Death has in their arsenal of weapons must and will be unleashed on them all. Trust me, the demons of hell are smiling because massive is their pay day because they are going to get paid.

You cannot sin reckless and rude and think Lovey is going to forgive you just like that.

You did all to displease him and bring him shame.

You allowed death to mock him.

You allowed death and his children to deceive you because no one can deceive God; Lovey, not even me.

You if you have children allowed death and the demons of hell to take your children as well as possess some of them.

All manner of evil humans did and expect to continue to have life. This cannot be hence we are judged by our sins and yes sentenced because of our sins. Billions of you your sins outweigh your good hence you are truly hell bound literally.

Michelle

Yes I get down on Lovey all the time. People we say Jesus is his son; child and look what humans did to him. They crucified him.

You in the religious community with the exception of Muslims say Lovey; sorry God gave us his child and we as humans slaughtered him worse than a pig. Now we have the gaul to say and expect Lovey, sorry God to save us.

We did not secure his child.

All in humanity murdered him then have the gaul to harp on him (Jesus) and say he's going to save all of you.

Unnu kill di man

Unnu gi di man bitta gaul mixed with vinegar to drink on di cross and Lovey fi figive all of humanity?

None a unnu stan up fi di man but yet want di man fi save all a unnu. Wow.

What bleeping nerve.

Who the bleep are any of you for Lovey to save?

<u>Unnu shed di man blood and until this day unnu a drink di man blood anna nyam im flesh.</u> (Communion and whatever nastiness you church goers do and still do). So if unnu still a drink di man blood anna nyam im flesh; how im a guh save any of you?

No tell me.

How Him a guh save any of you if you're all feasting on his dead and rotten carcass?

A suh fi him flesh suh sweet dat unnu live affa di man like scavenger?

Wow

My Peeps and Family, trust me, Lovey will never ever send his children and people in forbidden and unclean lands.

He refuses to send me to Jamaica.

He refuses to let me go into places he does not like. So truly think and stop letting the clergy fool you by taking your soul and or spirit and condemning you to hell with them. They (the clergy) need company in hell. Truly do not follow them. Save yourself come on now.

Michelle

Listen people, Lovey do warn us, we are the ones to not listen to him. We are the ones to sell him out. No, look at what they did to Jesus in your book of sin and death. **_Yes your holy bible is death's book. This is what death gave to his people to fool you and you believe in it._**

I've told you, Lovey does not deal in death because he is good and true life. I battle him but you cannot because you did not make Lovey your good and true friend. There is a bond of truth between us and no matter how I go up against him He knows I am truly there for him.

He knows of my unconditional true love for him because at times he feels it and he cannot say otherwise.

Stop letting the church fool you with the Jesus bullshit because no God would send their child to die for anyone.

Death wouldn't do it either, so truly think. Death is like this, they do not give up what belongs to them that easily.

Lovey is our ultimate source and he would never ever without a shadow of a doubt sacrifice any of his children and people for anyone. **_WHEN WE AS HIS CHILDREN AND PEOPLE INCLUDING_**

<u>MESSENGERS SIN, WE DIVORCE HIM BY BREAKING OUR BOND WITH HIM. OUR BOND IS OUR MARRIAGE TO HIM AND WHEN WE SIN, HE LET US GO. HENCE DEATH COMES TO TAKE US BY ANY MEANS NECESSARY.</u> We see this with Adam and Eve of your book of sin; death. You also see this with me. He is trying to save me by keeping me in his fold.

Lovey did warn them (Adam and Eve and he's warning me) not to do wrong and they disobeyed. Yes I am trying because it's hard for me walking with him. So I battle him Lovey by taking out all my frustrations out on him. I truly like it this way, hence I truly, truly more than unconditional truly love the relationship we have, but not the pain and suffering. So because they (Adam and Eve) disobeyed, Lovey gave them over to the choice they made. It's the same with us today.

Lovey has been trying and we are the ones to reject him. ***LOOK, YOU SAY HE SEND HIS SON TO US TO SAVE US, AND WHAT DID WE DO?***

He got slaughtered by humans and in death and or while on the cross of death, he was mocked because they gave him bitta gaul mixed with vinegar to drink. This according to your book of sin; death. Now if you did this to Lovey's child, how is he going to save you?

Did you not reject and slaughter his child?
Does the church globally with the exception of Muslims not feast on the man's blood and flesh?

So if you do this to the man, and it matters not if you say it's a spiritual thing and not an actual thing, you are still feasting on his blood and flesh. You practice this in the living and none of you can tell me otherwise. Hence cannibalism is worldwide. So with all this said and done by each and every one of you and once upon a time me because I was a church goer myself but never fit in. How can Lovey; Good God and Allelujah save any of you? I no longer do it, go to church and I did ask for forgiveness of my sin and sins, so I am truly good to go but you are not.

You are eating his son and drinking the blood of his child. You are not remorseful.

Don't you dare say you are not because each Wednesday, Saturday and Sunday sometimes Monday and sometimes Tuesday and Thursday you all go before God and eat the flesh of his son as well as drink his blood. YOU MOCK GOD AND EXPECT HIM TO SAVE YOU!!!! Please

You feast on his son and expect him to save you.

Lovey anno fool fi anyone come on now.

You do all to disgrace and discredit him and he's to say, Paul, Sandra, Carlos, Lita, Angie, Renée, Byron, Steven, Mark, John, Hezekiah, Blue, Marlon and Marcus, it's okay, I forgive you for what you've done to my child. I will overlook the fact that you mock me.

I will overlook the fact that you killed him and still killing him.

I will overlook the fact that you deal in human and animal sacrifice because you sacrifice my son when you accept communion; hence killing him over and over again. All this matters not to me because my son's life is not valued by me. Yours is, hence I give death authority; all he and she requires of me just to save you. Come on now. Wow. Allelujah.

Glory. Have mercy Lord.

Allelujah Lovey because you are more than worthy to be praised.

All that you as humans think and do to him; say he would do to save you the wicked and evil of this world, ***truly GOOD LUCK BECAUSE LIKE I SAID, LOVEY WILL NEVER EVER SACRIFICE HIS OWN TO SAVE THE WICKED AND EVIL.***

Evil know the evils they have done.

We have a choice and instead of making good choices for ourselves, we let the church conquer and divide us.

We give the churches globally the right to choose for us as well as choose your destiny. Well you not me. I made my good choice on my own hence I have no ties with the church except for Zion. *I still go into the HOUSE OF ZION IN THE SPIRITUAL REALM AND I TRULY DO NOT KNOW WHY.* Meaning I do not have the full truth of her in the living.

We allow the church to continue to lie to us. We do not think. Lovey is clean, why the hell would he allow dirty and unclean people to preside over you. You have to clean yourself up just like I did me. It's not easy walking with him but I am trying. So what makes you any different.

STOP LOOKING FOR A SCAPEGOAT BECAUSE LOVEY WILL NOT GIVE YOU ONE. You want life, then live life good and clean; true. Mistakes are there and we all make them (mistakes) including me. There are things I truly do not know and when I know them I will tell you. Learn from your mistakes and make them no more come on now.

NOT BECAUSE I AM WRITING FOR LOVEY DOES IT MEAN I DON'T GET LONELY AND FED UP. I DO, BUT I GO TO HIM AND YOU SEE THIS IN THIS BOOK AND OTHERS. I have issues just like you. I have aches and pain just like you.

I have financial hardship just like you. So truly don't think it's easy for me. *I MADE A COMMITTMENT TO HIM AND I HAVE TO KEEP MY COMMITTMENT NO MATTER HOW ANGRY I GET AT HIM AND TELL HIM I AM LEAVING.*

He will not let me leave and I truly love this about him. And yes, at times I do things to piss him off when I need a little attention from him and he knows this. You guys know this if you've read any of the other books in the Michelle Jean Series of Books.

At times I am spoilt and would truly, more than truly love it if he can spoil me each and every day with his goodness, true love and compassion. His blessings I have I know this, I just need to do more and accomplish more for him and yes me and you.

So live come on now.

You cannot murder Lovey's children and people if we are under his protection. When we leave his fold we give him up hence we are not protected by him.

I am no matter the hardship (s) I face. Some of my hardships has nothing to do with me. Meaning my children give me grief and cause me pain. Spirits do the same to me yes but I worry not about them. Like I've told you, there's a App for wicked and evil people and spirits including children, and that App is hell. So I worry not about my enemies. I know the fire that consumes the spirit so why would I worry about wicked and evil people including spirits. They have an end hence I know their end, so I let them be. I have no time for them.

You on the other hand truly do not know hence you have these books to teach and guide you. Yes they are laden with mistakes; typos but it cannot be helped. I've tried to make these books error free but unfortunately they are not.

And no I cannot bring anyone into the mix when it comes to these books. I have to write alone. It is only when that person is ordained to help me, then I will get help, but I truly doubt if anyone will be ordained to help me.

You know some of the truth now. Hence you are beginning to know life.

Truly live true and clean. **_"TRUTH IS EVERLASTING LIFE."_** So why not live truthfully. You want to live. There are no shortcuts to life. Lies cannot save you, only truth can.

Lies do not give life nor does lies beget life. Lies kill all including you.

So no one can say they are going to see Lovey (God) and have lies (sin) on their plate; record. And even if you have one sin on your plate and or record, you will not see Lovey (God) nor will you reside with him. You will however see the other god and that God is Death.

Michelle
June 14 and 18, 2015

It's June 13, 2015 and the back pain is back.

Man I can't take this lower back pain anymore. This is getting too severe.

My nights are filled with pain; so much pain and it's pretty bad.

How do I stop this pain?

I so need to see the doctor and have my lower back checked out because this pain I truly can't take anymore; it's too severe.

FAM, I AM READY TO GIVE UP ON GOD, GOOD GOD AND ALLELUJAH.

I am at my crossroad now where I cannot bare anymore suffering. It it's not one thing it's another with me.

Oh man this pain is unbearable. You just want it to stop but the pain won't stop. It just keep coming.

I have to walk away from Lovey now man because the bullshit I face in my life I can't take anymore.

It's like I am being abused.

It's like I am in an abusive relationship with Lovey. No one should feel abused come on now man.

Where is my road to happiness?
Where is my road to freedom?

All I see is death with him.

Death in the waking moments; death in my sleeping state and I truly cannot take it anymore.

I am alone in this hence I truly have to go my way and sever my ties with him.

I truly, truly, truly can't take anymore abuse literally.

No Fam, how can a god see your hardships and pain and leave you in your hardships and pain?

I am becoming broken again because I cannot handle the pain. I have no one beside me to rub my back for me.

No one to cry with me or even say it's okay dear I am with you. I am all alone going through this and I am tired now man. It's as if my life is cut off from the rest of the world and universe. Man what I wouldn't give for someone to put a hot rag or hot water bottle on my back right now.

My pain and suffering is there people and it's coming yet again. This time more brutal than ever. This is my daily life hence life with Lovey sucks.

I am so beginning to hate my life. Too much health woes; pain.

Too much financial stress.
Too much stress period.

Life here on earth stinks Lovey. It's not worth it given the amount of pain we have to face.

How much more do I have to go through before you release me from all my pain and agony; this hell hole I am in?

What is the point of choosing life when at times you wish for death due to pain and suffering?

You are an abuser.

No for real Lovey look at it. We choose life and this is what we get? Then keep life because neither you and death is worth it.

You cannot beat up the person for choosing you and I've been beaten.

I am still being beaten up and you're not doing anything to help me.

I am batta bruised literally, so what say you?

Your word isn't true then.

You beat us.
Death kills us.

Both of you work hand in hand.

Yes I cussed her and defended you when she said God kills and now I regret doing that.

You beat us; allow us to be beaten and killed because in truth you have no good will towards anyone but you.

You never wanted us in the first place hence you left us to die.

Michelle
June 13, 2015

And no I will not apologize to you for my statement because it's the truth. You have no good will towards me and your people. You wanted me to fail in all that I do hence you allowed; permitted the severe beatings in my life.

Truth does not cause pain.
Truth does not hand over his or her children to be slaughtered by the hands of death and his people.

Truth isn't weak when it comes to their own. Hence you are weak and without a spine.

You're not strong hence I've chosen the wrong god; side.

Look at me and see my hurt and pain.

Look at your people and see their hurt and pain. You keep us captive.

You keep us shackled and chained and I refuse to be your damned slave.

I refuse to be in an unhealthy relationship with you.

I am no longer begging you for anything because you cannot provide me with a damned thing.

My happiness counts.
My life counts.
My all counts.

All of this you truly know nothing about. Life isn't about hurt and pain but you hurt.

It's June 13, 2015 and I realize no God is worth it when you have to struggle and go through more than hell on the face of this planet.

Neither You or Death is worth it hence people walk away from you.

Yes I've seen things but what good is seeing things when seeing things come at a cost; a severe cost?

Yes through death we part but you make it so. You make it so hard for us that we do part from you. Hence you are to blame for many things.

In all you give you are not truthful nor are you fair.

Michelle
June 13, 2015

I did what you asked of me Lovey but it's time for me to move on.

As for your mega mansion please find someone else to build it or purchase it for you.

I've come to the end of my journey with you as human and spirit.

I have to respect myself hence I cannot stay in your abusive relationship anymore.

I refuse to walk on your lonely and deadly road anymore.

This road is a death trap filled with obstacles and pain.

So I encourage people to never ever take this road with you. I encourage them to live their life good and clean for them and not for you. Because in truth, you are truly not there for anyone. Goodness is within and to be honest Lovey you are truly not good.

No one that is trying to get to you should have to feel pain and this is why I say you are not good. Forget about sins for a minute.

We are coming to you.
Walking towards you.

Why should we and or anyone stumble and fall to reach you?

Why should anyone go through hardship to reach you?

Yes I am hurting because I am in so much pain and you can't ease my pain.

Not even a cup of tea you can make me.

Not even my back you can rub. So why should I continue to trust you and put all my trust in you?

It doesn't stop with you hence I have to break free and leave this abusive relationship with you.

Michelle
June 13, 2015

Yu noa yu wicked.
Don't smile because every negative words and anger I have to take out on you because I truly do not like this pain.

You are my backlash and I will not apologize this morning.

Why do I have to be in so much pain Lovey?

Why do I have to be alone in all of this?

Where is my comfort?

When and where does my help come?

Why abandon me in my time of need?

Something is so not right.

Why the hell do I have to go through sickness alone Lovey?

Why?

You hate me.
Why do you hate me?

Do you not see my needs; suffering.

Hence people do all not to get sick.

Take care of your mind, body and soul including spirit.

Sickness is a bitch, so truly take care of yourself.

Grow your own organic food.

Eat healthy and exercise regularly.

Try to stress yourself not.

Do not bring stress in your household, it will kill you and take all from you.

The pain is not worth it.

Things I used to do I can't. I feel trapped hence if I could escape this wretched land for someplace warm I would escape without looking back and without regret.

Michelle
June 13, 2015

Yes it's my day and I am feeling pain.

Wow

Man baby pain isn't as bad as this pain. No position is comfortable people. Hence my brutal writings this morning.

Trust me I can't even put Lovey in this position. And if I could, I wouldn't.

Yes I want and need him to feel what I feel but I can't, not this way but some other way.

My life is not his.

Pain sucks.
I truly hate pain.

It's not like when I was a kid I could tolerate it. I am way older and the older I get, my threshold for pain is greatly diminished.

I know suck it up and stop complaining, but I can't.

I am happy my head isn't hurting me like yesterday, but my lower back is killing me.

No position I go in help.

And yes you can say why should Lovey help you when you cuss him so?

You're right but it's not you feeling this pain I am.

I can't smile at my pain, it freaking hurts. It's not like the pain go and come. It's constant, not giving up.

I so have to lose some weight off my breasts and hips. Way too top heavy and hip heavy.

Michelle
June 13, 2015

Ah man there is so much more that I want to say but time will not permit me. Yes I took my anger out on Lovey this morning as you can see. The pain is subsiding now but I have to bare on despite what I told Lovey above.

It's unbelievable how people treat his son – well so called son and expect him Lovey to be all forgiving.

If Jesus died for our sins, would we not stop sinning?

If Jesus shed his blood for each and every one of us, why are we as humans defiling him and sinning? Why do we not respect what he has done for us?

We obviously do not respect him because if we did, there would not be so much sin and evil here on earth and in the universe.

Hence Lovey I've asked you before, if we do not have truth, will we not believe in lies and do all that is wicked and evil; sinful?

Yes you have to take the blame for some of the things that is happening on and or in earth.

You made a choice also.

You made a choice to permit us to allow sin into this world.

If you did not want sin and evil to get into this world; earth as well as into our genes, you would have made impenetrable frameworks and foundations with us; humans but you did not. Now look at humanity here on earth and how vile and wicked we have become.

Hence she came to me and told me God kills.

Yes I defended you but I now have to doubt you.

You cannot say you love us so and leave us unprotected when it comes to sin and evil. Yes we made the choice to sin, but many did not. Many have and has come to you and relinquished their sinful ways like me. *THE COST TO LIFE IS TOO GREAT LOVEY, HENCE LISTEN AND DO THAT WHICH IS GOOD AND TRUE; RIGHT AND CLEAN FOR US.*

Look at what I am going through right now.

Look at what billions of people are going through right now.

Many have made a good and conscious choice to follow you; walk with you, but yet you leave us to suffer. Why?

___Now I've told you yet again that I am leaving you and you rain dun hail pan mi.___

Lovey yu rightid when it comes to mi?

Listen, I more than unconditionally truly love you beyond measure, but are you sure you want to battle me?

Remember your temper is not as fierce as mine. So truly think because certain games I truly do not play not even with you.

I've told you time and time again I cannot take my health woes and you are not listening to me. The pain is too severe and I cannot take it. Yes the body is weak and sometimes my spirit gets downcast, but trust me my fierce will and strength is that strong and deadly. So truly don't when it comes to me and you in this way. I am not Eve (Evening). I come to you with all including my wrath and anger, so truly don't go there by raining down hail pan mi because *YOU ARE THE ONE THAT IS NOT LISTENING.*

I CANNOT ENDURE ANYMORE HARDSHIPS AND PAIN.

I CANNOT STAY IN AN ABUSIVE RELATIONSHIP WITH YOU. I CANNOT. I WILL TURN AGAINST YOU AND TRULY HATE YOU AND YOU TRULY DON'T WANT THAT BECAUSE I WILL DO ALL TO STRIP YOU OF EVERYTHING AND YOU KNOW THIS.

I'VE TOLD YOU, TRUE LOVE DO NOT CAUSE PAIN NOR DOES IT HURT.

LIFE; GOOD AND TRUE LIFE I TRULY LOVE HENCE I DO NOT PLAY AROUND WITH LIFE. I'VE TOLD YOU, YOU CANNOT PROTECT DEATH'S CHILDREN BECAUSE THEY DO NO RESPECT YOU NOR DO THEY CARE ABOUT YOU.

THEY WOULD RATHER KILL YOU; GOOD AND TRUE LIFE THAN MAINTAIN IT.

YOU ARE NOT A PART OF EVIL'S MANDATE. HENCE WICKED AND EVIL PEOPLE AND SPIRITS DO ALL TO DESTROY YOU AND YOUR PEOPLE WHICH IS OUR PEOPLE.

I'VE TOLD YOU, LET THE CHILDREN OF DEATH GO BECAUSE THEY DID NOT CHOOSE YOU. YES MANY OF OUR PEOPLE CHOSE DEATH, HENCE

THE BEATINGS WILL NEVER STOP FOR BLACK PEOPLE AND OR THE BLACK RACE.

DEATH'S PLAN WAS TO TAKE US AWAY FROM YOU BY ANY MEANS NECESSARY AND IT WORKED. SOME PEOPLE DID WAKE UP BUT BILLIONS ARE STILL ASLEEP. THEY DON'T WANT TO WAKE UP, SO YOU HAVE TO LEAVE THEM. THEY CHOOSE AND OR CHOSE TO SLEEP WITH DEATH SO LET THEM GO.

YOU ARE TARNISHING YOUR IMAGE AND YOU ARE ALLOWING AND OR PERMITTING ME TO CONTINUE TO DOUBT AND BATTLE YOU. I NEED THE DOUBT AND BATTLE TO STOP MORE THAN INFINITELY AND INDEFINITELY MORE THAN FOREVER EVER WITHOUT END. Come on now and listen. I cannot plea with you and to you anymore. Something has to give and I am giving. You are too reckless and dunkya.

Mi an death anno fren, so why do you constantly hurt me with death?

Why do you constantly ignore me?

Trust me if it's a battle you want I will give it to you but know I will not lose against you. I will not back down from you when it comes to my right and the rights of our good and true people.

As a father you have an obligation to us. Just as we as your children have an obligation to you.

I've given you my truth, why can't you do the same. I defend you, so defend me when it comes to death and their wicked and evil own.

Defend my health now man come on now. Don't leave me in pain and ruin.

You don't want to lose me but yet you are sacrificing my health and well being. Why?

I've told you, true love cannot hurt. Buoy yu good. Look how quick yu ready fi rain dung hail pan mi as mi sey mi a lef yu, but when it comes to helping me health wise and providing stability for me, you cannot do it.

So who's the hypocrite in all of this?

No, you are being a hypocrite. Yu nuh want mi fi leave, but you are allowing me to face pain and hardship. Wow.

No people and family you've read what I wrote this morning due to pain. I could not take the pain anymore. Yes my eldest son made me something to eat and he wanted to take me to the hospital but I did not want to go. If things get worse I will go. The lower back pain is gone but the pressure in the base of my head is coming. Not as severe as yesterday but I am baring on.

So after writing what I wrote, I fell asleep. In my dream it was raining on and off. Walking, it began to hail from the sky but not big hail, tiny ones. People the hail was coming down like rain; a downpour of rain but in this case hail. I said really an chap a bad word (swore) and the hail stopped. So yu si how quick Lovey jump eene because mi tell him mi a lef him. But look how long it teck im fi ease mi pain.

Look how long mi a complain to im bout mi health woes and financial hardships and as mi sey mi a lef, look wey im du to mi. So tell me just how fair he is to me?

Onwards I go. In the dream I walked to this area around 299 Queen Street and Ellen DeGeneres was there. I said to myself what was she doing here?

My mind was edging me to go up to her and ask her to help me with my books but I did not do it.

I left her alone and pretended like I did not see her. I wanted to take the bus and go home so I walked to the intersection where I could take the bus. I did not have enough change and I did not want to put bills in the money slot.

I asked someone where this bus went and this lady said Dundas Station. I can't remember what transpired but I believe mother said something and daughter said, "it's not so," and a big argument broke out with mother and daughter. This was while waiting for the bus people. Somehow I got change to take the bus but the coins some of them were green coins. Green is disappointment for me people. So I guess somewhere I am going to get disappointed with money. Nothing new to me hence I do not let my finances stress me out like it used to. Yes I still get stressed but I can only do so much. And besides I am use to financial failures due to her and what she did to me.

Getting the coins I moved away from the argument and this jet black horse appeared and started to jump on this lady and licking her. The horse saw me now and the jet black horse with legs that reminded me of a dog's feet (poodle) jumped on me and started to lick me on my face and on my mouth. It's as if he was sucking the life out of me. If you go to Google Images and type in poodle you will see some with pinkish skin and poufy fur. The horses feet and or hind legs was similar to this.

This horse people was no bigger than a pony and very young. I got annoyed and pushed the horse away from me. People, everyone wanted to kill this horse and we began to have negative thoughts. Ellen picked up on the negative thoughts and said, "such negativity." She also gave me this picture of this black man with a big afro. The young man or man was not attractive but ugly to me and on the side; left side of his head in the picture but not on his head was white etching. But what struck me was that the picture she gave me, the photo of the black man turned into a picture of a white man.

The man (white man) was medium to fat built in the face. His nose was not as fat. The picture changed and showed what looked like this man's brain that went from grey to off green. So the picture was constantly changing.

So if any of you can make any sense of this dream go right ahead because this seem to me like a dream in a dream.

I also dream DMR Zing Flash Films. The light skinned big mouth brother CV and Fox. Dreamt we were in this fast food place. Either McDonald's or KFC and we wanted hamony corn portage but they did not sell that. This lady (I believe she was Chinese) showed us the menu of what they sold. So CV and Fox wanted to buy bread. French Baguette bread and this other bread but he could not pay for it. So I told the man; tall black man behind the counter that I would pay for the bread and he said, "you're going to pay for the bread?" And I said yes. But it's so weird though. I could taste the portage in my mouth.

Weird

Hence my dream world is getting weirder and weirder.

Michelle
June 13, 2015

PS. There's a picture in Google Images by 22DOG.COM that resembles the jet black horse in my dream. People you see how the hind and or back leg of this dog is fluffy. Not the bottom fluff but the top fluff. This is what the feet of the jet black horse that is as small as a pony looks like. Yes I embedded the image but took it out because I've caused enough commotion in these books. I know some people are going to sue me for using their image but it cannot be helped.

I will not put anything into this book because I truly cannot decipher these dreams.

The black man turning into white just tells me his state in death. I've told you in some of my other books, that when wicked and evil people die, they die as white dressed in white. So in truth I am seeing this man's picture in his dead state and or when he is going to die in the spiritual realm.

Yes I am trying to find a picture of this man on the internet but cannot find it. Alright let me try this. Bounty Killer the dancehall artist had this artist he was backing but have since let go I think. He is quite dark and has a fro. He has this scar on his face and he is truly not attractive.

When I see this man I see death and I have wonder how many lives he's sent to never land in the living.

There is nothing attractive about this man. And to be honest some of di duppy bat Satanist that pree the devil better looking than this man.

I am sorry people but all I see is death in this man. Pure evil hence I truly do not see a clean light in him. And to you young man, this is what I see hence I have to speak the truth that is in and on my mind. I am not judging you, I am just telling you the hell I see in you. Sad yes, but many in Jamaica belong to the devil. Hence you the Jamaican people had better think twice because death has millions of you locked literally.

Michelle
June 15, 2015

Like I said, there is more that I would like to add to this book but I won't. I am going to leave this book as is because it is unfinished and I truly do not know if I am going to have a My Day Book Three.

If I do then this is good but I highly doubt it. I need to focus on Blackman Redemption – The Truth About Jesus but can't for some strange reason. I've written this book just about three years ago if not more but can't finish it. Maybe if and when I get to the Cayman Islands or Russia; if not Africa I will finish it.

It's not much I left out of My Talk Book Ten but here we go.

Michelle

It's June 08, 2015 Lovey and I truly don't know what to write right now.

Don't know what to write about us.
Don't know what to write about me.

No I am not drawing a blank but I just don't feel like writing.

I don't think I am at a loss for words; I'm just not into writing tonight.

Yes I want and need to do something different but what I truly don't know.

Oh man both dogs are looking at me for food.

I swear they don't look to anyone else for food in this way apart from me.

Yes I spoil them.
Treat them as one of my own.

Yes including the puppy who drives me crazy until this day.

She annoys me.

She doesn't make me sleep enough and she sheds like crazy.

Dog hair everywhere.

Ah Lovey, what a life when it comes to me.

Yes I have nothing of substance to write on this night.

Do I truly want to write tonight?

No

I just want to read.

Man I need to source out some more Zane books and cuddle up to them.

Ah but I truly need my own place to just relax and unwind.

And no, I so do not need the drama of a skirt or a shirt around me.

Too much stress and headache.

Michelle
June 08, 2015

Lovey I need to get away from family. Well no, my family doesn't stress me.

My niece on the other hand does not listen and she's always in a financial bind like me.

I have four kids and she has two and she's in a worse situation than me. I can't even put my hand on it.

Lovey I am so going to leave things alone. I cannot stress and or stress myself over my niece. I have other pressing issues that are causing me pain.

I know my head and the fluids that run to my brain, hence I cannot take on her problems right now.

Lovey I don't know about life anymore. I am struggling too hence I complain to you.

Ah Lovey, I leave all my troubles aches and pain in your capable hands as I look forward to the day when I am totally debt free and I can help; truly help others to ease their pain and burdens; suffering.

Life isn't easy Lovey for many of us hence I turn to you for hope and guidance.

Lovey you are the main influence in my life and I have to keep it so always.

One day Lovey
One day

One day I will be whole again and be free of all that ails and hinders me.

Michelle
June 08, 2015

Lovey it's June 09, 2015 and I have to ask what is the difference between you and her?

I've been trying for years but in all my trying, I've failed you and me including our people.

What I want and need to do I cannot do it and this is frustrating to me.

Now this morning I dreamt this young lady. She's black and she's downgrading Lulu. Lovey Lulu is where I need to be and you know this. Remember my dreams of leaving Lulu and the world was taken from me.

This company is where she needs me to be in terms of our books. So why is this young black lady or girl downgrading Lulu; complaining about them?

Lovey in the dream I told her I tried going mainstream and was rejected. I told her some self publishing authors have gone on to be signed and or picked up by major publishing house like the author who wrote fifty shades of gray.

Lovey why now after all these years is someone complaining and calling Lulu mickey mouse; not credible? Lovey this is someone in the spiritual realm.

Why is she knocking the choice I made and the choice she made for me?

Lovey, our work is not mickey mouse. Is she saying because Lulu is not credible in her eyes, our books isn't and or aren't credible either?

Wow that's all I can say.

Lovey we are not credible?

Is she saying because our books are not published by the big publishers no one can put value on the words that are written in them?

Lovey who is she to lambaste us?

Is she a writer and did you tell her to write a book not once but twice?

Michelle and Michelle Jean
June 09, 2015

Lovey a who shi?
Dis dry up fluxy ass gyal a cum bout Lulu a mickey mouse; not credible when it comes to publishing.

Lovey different people have avenues of choice. This is the choice I made and the choice made by her for me. So why would I not accept this road and continue on this road until I cannot continue on it (this road) anymore?

To interrupt the flow of this book. Fam, I know I have to leave Lulu one day. Remember what death and or sin said about America. Hence I too have to leave out of Babylon. Yes I know there are European and Canadian houses that print for Lulu but until that day comes, I am staying put until change comes. Yes I know the change but I have to see first.

Onwards I go.

Lovey yes I would have liked to have an editor and a publicist, but you've chosen none for me.

There is no help on your road for me I know this, hence I am the only one in your home.

When we are chosen we cannot bring someone else into the picture. We have to stay on your road no matter how lonely and boring it becomes for us.

So why is she casting doubt on the publishing house of my choice and her choice? Lulu is the

choice of Zion despite me wanting to leave sometimes.

Lovey I truly don't know hence I leave her in your hands because you know best.

Also dreamt Angelina Jolie and this man. Dreamt I was in this house. I went to go bathe but someone, a man bathe in the water and left the dirty water in the bath. So I let the water out but I did not have a rag to wash the tub out. So I used my hand and let water into the tub. The people in the house prior to me saying I am going to take a bath did not want me to. They said it was too late. It was about 11:30 at night and I could see their point, but I went ahead anyway. After washing the bath out and setting the water; this man walked by. He was white and a bit stocky with no shirt on. I pegged him to be European because he was white with pinkish red skin. I am not sure if he was Polish but he was definitely European to me. I wasn't naked but some of my clothes were off. Suffice it to say, I did not bathe because Angelina Jolie and this man were in the water. She had her arms around him and she was lovey dovey to him. It's like they were in love and dating. And no this man was so not Brad Pitt. I guess they were living together and he the man she was seeing was not faithful; he was a cheater. He had another woman on the side that dropped him home and she Angelina knew about this woman because she asked him if she dropped him home and he said yes. People I will not put anything to this dream because white dreams are funny and different.

White dreams could mean the opposite.
So I am so leaving this dream alone.

Dreamt Drake the Canadian rapper. Dreamt he was upset at me because I was taking a trip to Cuba.

He did not want me to go to Cuba because the United States banned people from going there. People I cussed him (Drake) out good and proper. I told him F the United States they can't tell me what to do. I told him I am not American but Canadian and America cannot tell us what to do; where to travel. Yes I took the trip because I was at customs and or in the customs area to check in for my flight to go to Cuba, and I made sure I was loud enough for the customs agent to hear me cuss out Drake.

The weird part of the dream was I had plane tickets in my bag, but none was for Cuba, nor did my plane tickets had dates on them and then it dawned on me that I did not purchase a ticket for Cuba. Strange.

I am so not going to read anything into this dream either because it seems I am missing something when it comes to my travels; my upcoming trip that I want to take.

Am I going to let this dream hinder me from going?
No I am still going until Lovey says otherwise.

Michelle
June 09, 2015

And Fam, if you feel as if there is something missing with some of the dreams I've given you, you are one hundred percent correct. In writing and or typing them, I was not into some of them.

Yes my dream world is weird and yes I am not into white dreams because of merit. I truly do not value them like I value black dreams. I guess it's because of lies and how white people lie and deceive billions on earth (religion and there so-called lying book called the holy bible) that they give to humanity so that they the people of earth can deceive self and go to hell and burn with them.

Listen I know death comes in both colours; black and white hence they work in unison; are related. One is physical and the other spiritual. Black is physical death while white is spiritual death. As humans we don't know this and now we and or you know.

Am I into this book fully?

No, because there is something lacking in it and I truly cannot put my finger on it. Hence I have to leave this book alone for what it is.

It's June 16, 2015 and I am so going to end this book before I get into more trouble, but before I go, dreamt Demi Lovato.

Dreamt she had 5 (five) videos that she was doing and to me (in the dream) she was not into the videos. She wore nice clothing. I believe she had a yellow floral dress with a flare on for one video and I believe a pink dress on for the next video. I can't remember if the pink dress had floral in it. But like I said she did not look happy and or into the video's. I told her she was not happy and she said, yes I am. People she did not look happy, she looked depressed as if she was lying to herself when it came to her happiness.

So you figure it out. Because friendship is no reason for anyone to stay in a situation they are not happy in. ***SOMETIMES WE TAKE CARE, THAT LITTLE PIECE OF COMFORT SOMEONE GIVES US AND FALL IN LOVE WITH PEOPLE THAT WAS ONLY THERE TO HELP US THROUGH OUR GIVEN SITUATION.*** I know Tyler Perry has a skit on this. All too often we become vulnerable and instead of just learning our lesson from that person we stick around and or fall in love with them. (Tyler Perry)

So she must know what she is doing because at the end of the day, depression is real and it does kill. Self punishment is a sin, hence no one should have to punish self for the pain we are feeling and or the pain that others cause us. Yes at times it's hard to get over the pain and hurdle but it does not mean we have to stay in situations that are unhealthy.

I don't want to stay in this unhealthy relationship with Lovey but he won't let me leave. I don't know if better comes for me with him but I guess I have to wait and see where his road lead me. Yes in life there are bumps and pitfalls in the way and it's hard to endure but do like I do. Make Lovey your true friend and let him help you. I know many of my troubles and a lot of them has to do with my children, hence I have to let them go on their own so that they can learn life and see just how hard life is. I can no longer sacrifice myself including health for them (my children) because some are truly not learning. Because I truly love them, I try to give them the easy way like Lovey has done to and for us. But like us, they want life the hard way and I truly don't know why. So yes I have to give them the hard way.

I've had a lot of dreams and I don't think I am going to get to them all.

Dreamt, this black man. I am going to say Jamaican because I think it's only in Jamaica that we make this juice and I could be wrong.

Dreamt he was making juice, pineapple juice but not the pineapple juice you get in a can. This pineapple juice is different. You could see him peel the skin off the pineapple and put it to the side. Someone asked him why he does not use the skin of the pineapple in the juice. He said he use the skin with the bark of the cherry tree to make a different kind of juice. A couple and or one of the skin of the pineapple fell on the ground and he picked it up. He moved to another area and I woke up out of my sleep before he could tell me what this juice and or remedy is used for. And for those who are asking, the juice remind me of the colour of a pina colada. When I think of this dream, I think of the cherry juice you can get at the side of the road in Jamaica that is homemade.

Dreamt pirates; men that looked like Somali pirates high jacked this boat. Man did they ever highjack the wrong boat. This white man and his wife was on the boat and this man was very powerful but these pirates did not know this. People and fam, this dream scared me so much because the man these pirates high jacked was that powerful but these pirates did not know this like I said. They did not know that all the man had to do was send a signal into space and all of them would be killed instantly. That was the part that scared me, knowing that this man could do this. Trust me I woke up out of my sleep immediately because I did not want to see the death of these men.

Hence I have to wonder if someone has the technology to use satellites to kill. But then, this is a ignorant and childish assumption of me given the advancement of technology today.

OH BEFORE I GO ON, DEXTA DAPS I DID NOT GET TO, WILL PROBABLY GET TO HIM IN MY BOOK BLOG.

BUT PEOPLE, CHECK OUT TRIPPLE A FOR ME. I HAVE TO HARP ON THIS GIRL BECAUSE SHE IS GOOD. BIG UP YUSELF TRIPPLE A, MI MORE DAN RATE YOU WHEN IT COMES TO YOUR FREE STYLE.

PROMOTORS PLEASE GIVE THIS GIRL A BREAK. YES SHI BIG BUT GUESS WHAT, SHI A DU HAR TING AND MI TRULY LIKE HAR.

Now Tripple A, do not come dirty, keep it clean for me because I truly don't know why the dancehall females have to come x-rated and crabbit. Most of dem. No let me leave my comments for my book blog where I can come rude and feisty.

Remember Tripple A do your thing clean. You have my props, please don't let me down. Fluffy to di wurl mi sey. Yu cute.

Mi like yu.

Plus you have an infectious smile about you. You go girl.

Tripple A, brap brap.

Bugle, mi a watch yu, yes I do not like you using swear words and I don't know why because I swear and cuss in some of these books. I guess maybe because I have high expectations of you.

Also, yu dark eene. Hence mi naah guh touch di ras inna da way deh. Oman nuffi touch. Wow. Mi like yu fi dat because yu clean inna da way dey.

Back to my dreams.

Dreamt it began to snow real hard this morning (June 16, 2015). And I was saying, how come it's snowing in June. This is unheard of. People and fam, in the dream all you could see was cars skidding and going in the grass. Some were trying not to hit each other. While all that was going on my puppy pooed and pied up my balcony for which she did and my eldest son told me it rained all night last night. I told him I was dreaming about snow. Weird.

Also dreamt I went to a baseball game. Toronto Blue Jays game. People I don't know how to give you a play by play of this dream. Just know Roberto Alomar was playing in the game, he was young. Pandemonium was on the field; because fighting broke out that really upset me. People I said this is not like baseball back in the day when Devon White and Joe Carter played. This type of baseball was disrespectful. People you could see the taunting of pitchers, the loaded base triple play but the bases weren't loaded. It was the pitcher throwing the ball to first base trying to get that player out and the first baseman miscued with the ball, hence the ball ended up coming in my direction. That was when pandemonium stated and every player was on the field fighting.

Yes I am worried because I use a lot of pictures in these books hence wow.

Will people sue me for using their pictures in these books without permission?

Many will; this is the facts and or reality of life. I do not use anyone's picture to make a profit. Beauty I like hence I promote your craft in these books. Pictures I use for you to see what I am talking about whether those pictures are negative or good.

Some things I just come across and or being led there for you to see and get the message. So if your craft is being promoted and people are seeing you, yeah me, I've done my job.

And yes if someone can perfect some of the images of the dreams I've told you about in these books; then go right ahead. Put them up on Google and or create a book. Hey you can call it, perfected and or pictures of Michelle Jean's dreams. ***And no, no compensation I require.*** Do your thing. Hey a copy of your book will do. No, I'll purchase it. So truly do your thing.

So yes I am stressing about being sued but you know what, I leave all in Lovey's capable hands. You know what certain things look like; it's up to you now to live your life good and clean.

Also, the cover of this book is important to all who are walking on the pathway of truth.

Yes I know I've used this cover before hence today, June 16, 2015 is the day I found out just how important this cover and or image is.

Dreamt that when you are walking on the pathway of truth and or to God, Good God and Allelujah, we are his light on his road and or highway. And people I don't think my wording is

correct because I cannot explain this road properly. But let the image on the cover of this book do the talking for me because it explains our journey very well.

<u>We are Lovey's light people.</u>

<u>We are the light of him in all the good and truth that we do. So please don't lose this light because this light is you.</u>

You are key to his happiness and existence. Yes I know billions do not belong to him but you do. I am no longer alone anymore because I can see you, His light on his road of truth.

So truly thank you from the depths of my heart for making this possible. I need you to continue on your true journey because light is there and that light is all of you. His chosen people and or his chosen few.

So yes the message is delivered so truly let us journey home together. Let us continue to be with him because in truth, the time of evil is over and it's time for us to walk home to him.

Maybe this is also why the white man was telling me to come home. Maybe my trials and tribulations are over and it's now time for me to start anew with me and you.

Like I said, we are his light on his highway and or road, so let's complete this journey, his journey hand in hand. So as I take your hand, we will make it because we are now together. We are no longer alone.

I am no longer alone.

So the preparation must now begin because like I said, my days are limited here on earth.

I have to prepare good places for you because death is going to come and take his and her wicked and evil own.

It's like I was watching On Stage yesterday (June 16, 2015). I viewed different artists but the artist that stood out most to me was Ky-Mani Marley. Not for what he said, but for the picture he instilled and left in my head. If you go to YouTube and type in ALL THE WAY, scroll through the video to where he showed you this beautiful coconut grove and or plantation. Man if only I had a picture of this plantation and or coconut grove. Simply breath taking hence I have to talk about it. And to be honest with you

I never knew this type of beauty existed in Jamaica. Portland is beautiful yes, but this natural beauty that exist in my homeland I truly did not know existed.

Wow

Hence I have to ask you the Jamaican community yet again, what happened?

Why did we give us this natural beauty to become as the lost?

We had Lovey's name.
We had his blessings and gave it up for what?

Look at what Jamaica has become now.

Look at the bloodletting on the land. 5 (five) bullets inna one man head. Unnu execute di man to regile and empty unnu magazine inna di man head; an none a unnu nuh si nothing wrong inna dat?

No, WI CRY OUT TO ALLELUJAH FI MERCY BUT LIVE LIKE THE MERCILESS.

WI CRY OUT TO ALLELUJAH FI JUSTICE BUT YET LIVE LIKE THE UNJUST.

TRULY LOOK AT THE HAPPENINGS IN JAMAICA RIGHT NOW AND TELL ME IF EVERY JAMAICAN ISN'T TO BLAME. Hence I put you on the list with Nigeria and Germany now. I will not save any of you because YOU ARE THE ONES TO CONDEMN JAMAICA DEN TUN ROUNE ANNA ASK GOD FI SAVE UNNU.

Lovey do not and will not save the unjust and merciless. Unnu kill wuse dan hog an unnu expect Lovey to look upon unnu with pity and mercy. Please.

TAKE A GOOD LOOK AT WHAT EVERYONE A UNNU DU TO LOVEY AND THE GORGEOUS ISLAND HE HAS AND HAVE GIVEN YOU. DI MAN, MY SWEETHEART AND UNCONDITIONAL LOVE OF TRUTH, GAVE YOU HIS NAME AND KINGDOM AND ALL OF YOU CONDEMNED IT WITH YOUR KILLINGS, BEHEADINGS, ABUSE, INCEST, RAPE, MERCILESS MURDERS. Now di oman dem inna dancehall a parade roune like prostitutes dancing for a meal in the courthouse and houses of whores and fools.

Everyone a dem a pat it up anna chat bout dem ha good up good up hole and how man want dem. In truth, some a dem truly need fi tek a good look inna di mirror because some a dem true decent man no want. Annu a such clowns that the global community look down pan black women; true black women and black beauty.

Revout sketels done pass some a unnu.

Nuff a unnu a merry go rounds fi man an unnu think this is nice.

Low class and no class, and yes nuff a unnu are talentless. Hence unnu sell unnuself to the highest bidder fi a likkle piece a dry bread. No, not dry bread, whatlef. Wey unnu boss nuh want. Unnu come eene worse dan di whatlef wey dey pan table, hence unnu a nyam an lef. Wey unnu boss an man throw to the dogs, no hogs.

Have some damn pride and ambition fi unnu self. Stop misrepresenting the true black women of this globe because they do not sell themselves cheap.

Many live in private, hence unnu a di one dem wey mek some a wi ole wi head down inna shame and disgrace.

And yes people I've opened up a can of whoop ass now. But facts are facts. I am so sick and tired of some of these women. So Tripple A once again, truly do not disappointment and keep your DJing clean. You go hard and fierce and I like that with you. Become the strong black woman you are meant to be. You don't need sex and dutty lyrics to sell you, so please do not sell your womanhood short.

Elevate, because it's not everyone that likes ghetto trash lyrically.

Not all poky can ole a man, so know what you are doing.

I like you hence I am plugging and pushing you. Mi big tu hence we fluffy an sweet.

I know a lot of you say I plug my Jamaican own too much and you know what, mi a Jamaican and despite me not saving them somehow deep down within I am still holding out for a beautiful and gorgeous change for Jamaica and Jamaicans. Yes death wants this land due to wickedness and yes Lovey did deem the island unclean, but my true heart is still with them despite the wickedness of them. No I will not defy Lovey. He needs his mega mansion in the Cayman Islands and he must get this ***BECAUSE THE GATHERING MUST START FOR HIS GOOD AND TRUE PEOPLE.***

Time is of the essence and in truth I know blacks and whites are going to reject me and frown upon me but that's okay. Many will call me a fraud and a liar and this is fine because I remember the time of Noah in your so called holy book. I truly don't care what you think of me. As long as Lovey, Good God and Allelujah truly loves me and defend me I am good to go.

I am not here to win a popularity contest with anyone. SO FOR ALL THE TRUE JEWS OUT THERE GLOBALLY. YES YOU LOVEY'S TRUE AND RIGHTEOUS PEOPLE, WHEN I SAY IT'S TIME AND OR THE GATHERING IS HERE; YOU HAD BETTER BE PREPARED TO LEAVE.

So start preparing from now. AND NO I TRULY DO NOT NEED YOUR MONEY OR HOUSE OR CAR.

It's not wha?

YOU HEARD ME. I DO NOT NEEN YOUR MONEY OR HOUSE OR CAR. YOU HAVE FAMILY, CHILDREN, GOOD FRIENDS, SO SAVE IT FOR THEM BECAUSE RIGHTFULLY THEY ARE YOUR TRUE LOVED ONES.

You are too.

I know I know but think of them (your family) also.

What I need you to do for me is create dialog for these books. PUSH THEM BY GENERATING SALES FOR US NOT ME ALONE.

Lovey needs his mega mansion so truly help me to give it to him. We need a place for us, so help me to help you also. Lands have to be bought and houses have to be built. So truly think. It's not Lovey alone I have to prepare for, I have to prepare for all of you also.

Hold my hand and never let go do you hear me. Let's be each other's strength because I refuse to leave anyone that belongs to Lovey behind.

Where I go you have to go.
Where I lodge you have to lodge. Eee coulda bi on di floor, wi a go lay pan di floor together. I have to prepare for all of you, so help me up and never help me down. (Ruth)

I am not here to rob you because you've all heard this all before. Plus you do not know me. I am just like you and don't think I do not have blemishes on my plate. My past is there for you to read and see. Ask about. I refuse to lie to you about anything; hence we must have total truth amongst us. Yes you can hate me.

You don't have to like me.
You can doubt me.

No, you can't kick me in the ass or knock me down because I bruise very easily.

I know trust is earned and over time I hope I will have your trust. This does not mean if I am doing wrong you can't say, watchya dutty gyal or Mitch yu du disya wrong an mi nuh like eee. Hence truly be my good keeper in all that I do.

I need you family and so does Lovey. So let's work in unison and build good and clean; true and right for Lovey, so that he can join us.

He's ready and trust mi, mi more dan ready like Freddy so truly do not disappoint me and Him.

Yes Lovey.

Hence to the true BLACK RACE WHETHER WHITE BLACK OR CHINESE, IT'S TIME TO PREPARE TO LEAVE BABYLON INDEFINITELY.

IT'S TIME GO HOME. SO PREPARE YOURSELF. DO NOT MISS YOUR CALLING LEST YOU GET LEFT BEHIND.

Michelle and Michelle Jean
June 16, 2015

Wow.

Dear God what is going on in PNG?

I thought I was finished with this book but Lovey, dear God is this what the black race is reduced to?

My God, Dear God I truly don't know what to do because my anger is boiling.

Why is the black race being slaughtered globally and you are not doing anything about it?

Lovey have mercy man when it comes to the people of PNG. You cannot let the unjust slaughter; continue to slaughter these people for their land and riches.

Have mercy man come on now. Dear God did you see the images of these people lying dead. This is what the Indonesian Army is doing to these people and you stand there and approve this. The fucks are massacring Black People and taking their wealth from them and you allow this?

You allow Black People, our ancient people to be murdered like hogs. Was not the black babies that were fed to alligators enough, now this? Dear God man have some mercy and compassion on the black race. These are our people of old come on now and look at them.

America helped in all of this!

America helped Lovey, this is unbelievable. What more and how much more of our own should die by the hands of the wicked and unjust?

How much demons are you going to allow to slaughter and kill us. I defend you man come on now. This is more than wicked by the Indonesian Army man come on now.

I want to lash out at you brutal hence I am listening to FOR YOU by Kenny Lattimore to cool my temperament.

Good God man MURDER, DEM A MURDA BLACK PEOPLE, DO SOMETHING. MURDA, MURDA, MURDA. GOD A MURDA, DEM A MURDA WI PEOPLE AND YOU ARE ALLOWING THIS TO HAPPEN.

How much more man, how much more. Fuck man how much more of us should die before you step eene. Murda, Dear God murda, di demons of Indonesia a murda yu people dem. Murda.

Dear God, Murda.
Murda

Dem a murda wi people, Woooooo Murda, di murdarra dem loose.

Mercy, Allelujah, Mercy fi di Black people dem inna PNG.

Mercy Lovey, mercy.

My body and spirit is weak now.

Allelujah Mercy, mercy, mercy Lovey, Mercy.
Woo Allelujah; we need justice now man come on now.

Please Lovey help the Black People of Papua New Guinea because they need you.

Lovey, Dear God man, no. Another race a kill wi people dem hence I have no mercy for Indonesia.

None will be given to me by them because they take lives without regret.

No man. Look at the wickedness of America. Dear God man, Murda, murda.

Murda, murda.

America di wicked must fall because dem condemn and you Lovey allow this wicked and evil nation to stand.

Blood dey pan dem han. Murda dem a murda black people and we as black people cannot learn. Murda, di blood of these people I put on the heads of every America globally, hence America and Americans are condemned; must be condemned because they kill, sacrifice others for profit and you Lovey are to blame.

You are to blame hence I put the death of these people and the blood that was spilled; their blood in your hands. You continue to let wicked and evil people rein.

You continue to allow blood to be spilled. Hence I put the deaths and the blood of every black person including child and spirit that has died squarely on you. You owe them.

Vindicate them because if you let America and Indonesia go unpunished in all of this, then you will be dead to me.

Wickedness, Murda, dem a murda black people hence I leave the deaths and the blood of every child that was fed to Alligators in America, the United States of America and the slaughtering of everyone that died in PNG in your hands.

You cannot wash your hands clean of this Lovey because Blood is now in your hands.

Vindicate them. No Indonesian must go unpunished. It's blood for blood in my book due to anger and this I ask forgiveness from you for.

Life is worth it.

Come on now man, do something.

How can you as God sit there and do nothing?

How much more of us should die?

See the blood because you have it in your hands. You're dirty now because I've put the lives and spirit of these people in your hands and ask you with sincerity and truth for justice.

I put my life in your hands and ask you with sincerity and truth for justice. Look at what she did to me. Look at what he did to me. Look at the slaughtering of blacks globally.

I know we are not all your people but I am making them your concern.

I am taking up for them despite their beliefs and customs. No one should slaughter another race for land and gold, luxury. The gold and land rightfully belong to these people; **_hence blood is on every Indonesian hand._** I will not forgive them for the slaughtering of people for what rightfully belongs to them and every land that participated in this, including the United Nations and the United States of America if they are truly involved, I put the deaths and blood of these people on them, squarely in their hands because they were unfair and unjust.

None will ever see you if I can help it. Not even their children's children because condemnation is on them more than infinitely and indefinitely come on now.

Lovey yes I let my anger get the best of me but I want to curse everyone that has participated in this more than genocide infinitely and indefinitely without end for their part in this.

I want to curse death and the demons of hell for unleashing their demonic seeds on the black race.

When does the slaughtering stop?
When do we as black people wake the fuck up and learn that we are the targeted race for death?

When are we going to respect you and what you have given us as a token of your friendship and truth; true love?

When are we going to stop disrespecting self and have some fucking self worth globally and respect?

We are not animals. We let these fucks into our land. We gave them a fucking home when they had none and look at what they are doing to us.

When does it stop Lovey, hence I refuse to lift her curse of the white race. Fuck them and let them all go to fucking hell and burn, rot.

I denounce them from the black race.

Yes I am angry and truly forgive me for my anger. And yes I take back the denouncing of white people from the black race. And yes I take back my refusal to lift the curse of white people. Please forgive me yet again but it angers me how humans slaughter each other and steal everything from the black race. Yes my anger is geared towards the Indonesian government and army and I am truly sorry white people that I took my anger out on you alone. So Lovey duly note my remorse and truly

do not condemn all in the white race due to my anger because in truth, it would not be fair or just. Remember the good ones because my anger was based on hue alone, hence it has no merit nor is it warranted in this book.

But when does it stop Lovey?

When does the conquering stop?

When does the hatred stop?

When does the bloodletting stop?

When does my anger stop?

How would these people feel if death slaughtered their greedy and barbaric asses at will?

How would they feel if death swooped down and massacred them all without a care?

Yes an eye for an eye. But in this case what if death takes ten thousand for every black man women and child they slaughter and kill unjustly. They murdered senselessly, now tell me how the hell would they feel if death did this at will to their barbaric and unjust; murderous asses? Now I am truly weak Lovey. Yes I am angry hence I truly ask you for forgiveness for my anger. I will not ask them for forgiveness because I told you; I put the blood of these people in your hands and ask that you vindicate their deaths.

How the hell would they feel if Mother Earth took away every fruit, cattle, herb tree, and grass from them?

How the hell would they feel if every river, lake, sea, stream, pond, every drop of water was taken from them and their land and lands was left barren worse than all the desserts of the lands of earth?

How would they feel if every disease and locust infested their condemned and forsaken lands?

How would they feel if all life was taken from them without end?

None would like this, but yet they murder at will without cause and remorse; justification; greed.

Yes Lovey I have an evil side of me, hence you know what, no Indonesian is worth it in my book because they kill at will and steal what does not belong to them. Hence their land will lay in ruin indefinitely just like the United States of America because every person they kill whether good and evil has condemned them for their wickedness towards them. I now show you the souls and spirit of these people and put their blood in your hands for justice.

You can no longer be unjust because like I said, blood is now in your hands because I put it there.

You can no longer protect the wicked and evil of this earth and universe because the blood and spirit of the many cries out to you. The blood of the many flows like blood on the lands of earth globally.

You can no longer continue to permit evil to control, dominate and kill. You are wrong hence see the blood flowing before you. It is yours hence the seas of life turns to blood in many lands. These are the souls of humans that have been killed senselessly by the wicked and evil of this world globally. You now have it so do something.

You as Lovey and Good God have an obligation to Life, good and true life hence Psalms One. You can no longer let our good and true people live amongst the wicked. Yes I am wrong in my condemnation due to anger, but I will not change this. We cannot say we are humans; humane and massacre each other like this.

THE LAW SPECIFICALLY STATES, "THE WAGES OF SIN IS DEATH BUT TRUTH IS LIFE ETERNAL."

GIVE DEATH HIS AND HER WICKED AND EVIL PEOPLE. DO NOT STAND IN THE WAY OF DEATH. IT IS THE LAW. YOU CAN NO LONGER HINDER DEATH FROM TAKING HIS AND HER WICKED AND EVIL OWN.

Condemnation is on land, so do the right thing and step aside from the wicked and evil of this earth. YOU ARE CAUSING ANGER AND YOU ARE CAUSING ME TO GET ANGRY.

I truly do not want and need to see these things hence the human and animal sacrifices must stop. Your good and true people must walk away from death's people more than infinitely and indefinitely more than forever ever without end.

The laws are before you and you can no longer neglect them. If you do, you are wrong and guilty of sin just like man.

I am sorry but I have to do this. You can no longer let earth be the hiding place for evil.

You can no longer give the wicked and evil of earth a home.

You can no longer support them because they kill at will hence they have no remorse.

They have no respect for life and more importantly, they have no respect for you.

You cannot let the guilty go free anymore.

You asked me to do a job then be FAIR IN YOUR DEALINGS WHEN IT COMES TO ME, YOU AND OUR GOOD AND TRUE PEOPLE.

I will not stand for injustice hence I told you I will battle you for goodness and truth.

I will defend all that is right and clean. You are my more than my true love and you are capable of the truth, hence these death I put in your hands and hold Indonesia, the United States of America, The United Nations and all who participated in this more than genocide guilty as charged. All their names must go in the book of Judges to be judged and sentenced.

None must escape this injustice.

You have the truth before you.
You have the deaths before you.
You have the pictures on the internet before you.
You have this book before you.

You have my anger before you.

You have my cry before you.
You cannot let anyone of them go free because if you do, then you will as guilty as them.

And yes Lovey I know we've all sinned. You have my sins before you but I cannot sit down and watch injustice happen without crying out to you.

Lovey, Nelson Mandela came to mind. Look at what white South Africans did to him. Come on now man, when are you going to vindicate the black race and wake them up so that they can walk to you and with you in truth once again?

I know many cannot be saved. But do something. I have to come to you with my anger.

I have to put the blood of the people in PNG in your hands.

Lovey, you know the genuine and true love I have for life.

You know the genuine and true love I have for the trees and waterways, lands of this earth.

You know the genuine and true love I have for the environment.

You know the genuine and true love I have for the universe. All that is good and true, I have genuine and true love for.

You know the genuine and true love I have for you more than unconditionally. Not even the universe have this much true and unconditional love I have for you.

You know me when it comes to your fruits and food including waterways. I truly love them and you, so why hurt me like this?

Why?

Is this your way of angering me for saying I want to leave you?

Lovey, my greatest fear is losing you, but I will not sit down and see injustice.

I have to come to you with my anger and take it out on you like I've said.

Why give wicked and evil people a home if they are not going to respect your good and true life?

Why give wicked and evil people free rein if they are going to control and kill because of greed?

You see this happening globally but yet you leave people to be slaughtered. So tell me what is good and true life worth to you?

LOOK AT MY ANGRY STATE AND DO THE RIGHT THING.

DO THE RIGHT THING FOR THE PEOPLE OF PNG.

DO THE RIGHT THING FOR ALL WHO HAVE BEEN SLAUGHTERED.

You cannot permit thieves to continue to kill and take what truly do not belong to them. Hence I am coming to you for justice.

And if I have sinned in any way with my anger in this book, truly forgive me but truly let justice prevail.

Also Lovey, because I came to you in anger and pain with what is happening in PNG and finding out America, the United States of America is involved in this, I withdraw my petition to you in good faith to feeding the homeless of LA. I cannot in good faith and truth feed these people. Hence I withdraw my petition to feed them. I cannot see the injustice unto others by this nation and then turn around and feed and clothe their homeless. I cannot do it. Truly forgive me but I too have to be fair and just.

Hence I cannot feed these people nor will I petition you for this land. Hence every black land has and have destroyed not only you, but others including self.

How can a nation say they have GOOD AND TRUE LIFE; YOUR EYE IN THE TRIANGLE AND MOCK AND DISGRACE YOU LIKE THIS.

HOW CAN A NATION SAY IN GOD WE TRUST, BUT SLAUGHTER, DESIGN WEAPONS TO KILL AND KILL OTHERS SAY THAT THEY TRUST YOU. Yes I cuss you and cast doubt on you when I am angry and in pain, but this I cannot accept.

Now I must go back to the Jesus story. I now comprehend why they said Jesus was crucified amongst a murder and a thief. Hence the three deaths and or the three sons of death.

A LIAR
A THIEF
AND A MURDERER

All three are death hence the children of sin.
No Lovey be realistic here. This man claimed to be your son, but yet humanity crucified him on

a cross. This is supposed to be your child. ***THUS THE ENTIRE CHRISTIANIC (YES SATANIC) COMMUNITY MOCK YOU.***

MOCK YOUR CHILDREN AND MOCK LIFE.

You are of no worth to them hence they walk around with their religions of lies deceiving and killing people.

You know Lovey, I thought things would be different between me and you but they aren't. I thought all evil would disappear and vanish right away.

I had so much hope but to see this, the way the people of PNG are treated. Lovey, I saw the dead bodies on the internet.

These are black people Lovey.
What if the shoe was on the other foot?

You gave us wealth and strength and now look at us. We are being slaughtered for what rightfully belongs to us.

So tell me, when did one nation become so vile and wicked that it must arm nations to kill; exterminate another race?

When did the devil become the head of your people and household Lovey?

When did we truly stop walking with you?
When did we truly lose you?

Lovey, look at the dead bodies and tell me if this was justified.

Look at the Indonesian Army men kicking these people. They put their dirty feet on them. Where is the respect?

Hence I have no respect for Indonesian people period. They can all rot in hell if all I care. Hence if a earthquake was to hit that land and I had my last dollar I would not give it to them. I would rather spit on that dollar and use it to wipe my ass rather than give it to them. Fuck them because what fucking goes around comes around. And if one prayer of mine was to save them, I would close my mouth and mind from that prayer rather than save them.

Who the fuck are they to do this to another human being?

PNG is black land not Indonesian land, hence curse their murderous asses more than infinitely and indefinitely without end.

Yes I know descent and I wanted to bring descent into this but you will not allow me to. Hence none in Indonesia can use the descent bly.

None can say they are descendants of China or Mongolia or Russia or India because the descent law is closed to all Indonesian.

Hence they are locked out of your kingdom and abode indefinitely more than forever ever in my book. They are like unto the Babylonians and Ethiopians of old and today when it comes to me.

You don't slaughter people that have done you nothing.

You don't steal someone's land and say it is yours.

You don't enslave people come on now. Hence many lands in Africa are going to feel it because they too have done wrong. Many have and has slaughtered their own and steal their lands. Hence I plea the cause and case of the Bushman of Africa Lovey. I come before you in goodness and in truth again for these people.

Namibia and Botswana woe be unto your asses because you've stolen lands that do not belong to you.

You've driven your own out and treat them unfairly for what? These are your people and you slaughter them like animals. Steal their land and for this I truly hope Lovey do not forgive you for. You massacre and steal from your own. Hence Mama Africa is tired of her wretched and wicked own. You do not respect Africa, hence you're all liars and thieves; murderers. You've brought shame to Mama Africa and none of you look at me because you all know my past and present. (Behind the Scars)

You also know I am hot headed when it comes to injustice. I do not go to man's lying courts; I go directly to Lovey, Good God and Allelujah himself.

You've driven them (the Bushman) out of their homes and still doing it. Hence condemnation must take your lands for the evils you have done unto your own because of greed. HENCE YOU HAD BETTER DO RIGHT AND CORRECT YOUR SINS WHEN IT COMES TO THE BUSHMAN OF

AFRICA. YOU ERRED THEM, THUS YOU HAD BETTER BEG FOR FORGIVENESS AND RESTORE WHAT RIGHTFULLY BELONGS TO THEM. TRUST ME, IF YOU DO NOT DO RIGHT, WORSE WILL HAPPEN TO AFRICA BECAUSE I WILL MORE THAN CRY OUT MURDA FI DEM (THE BUSHMAN PEOPLE OF AFRICA). And no, I am not threatening your land. Do right by your people because what you are doing to them (the bushman people) is based on greed and truly unfair. Remember, Lovey gave Africa wealth and strength as well as a chance to redeem self, and all of you turned from your true ancestry. Hence condemning your own and refusing Lovey until this day. You continue to do wrongs HENCE MAMA AFRICA CONTINUES TO GET BRUTAL BEATINGS. Look at Africa as a whole and tell me why Africa has been reduced to more than rubble? Tell me why Mama Africa's children have and has been reduced to more than paupers?

HENCE LOVEY, EVERY POLITICIAN THAT TREAT THEIR PEOPLE UNJUST AND UNFAIRLY; TAKE THEIR NAMES OUT OF YOUR BOOK OF LIFE. FROM THEY ARE WICKED AND UNJUST, VILE AND MURDEROUS; NONE OF THEIR NAMES MUST BE ENTERED IN YOUR BOOK OF GOODNESS AND TRUTH BECAUSE THE LOTS OF THEM HATH NO TRUTH. THEY ARE ALL WICKED AND EVIL.

Further, let none petition for any of them.

You cannot say you govern your people and be unfair and untrue to them.

You cannot say you love your people but yet make them go hungry and without a proper place to sleep; live.

Hence I tell you Lovey, I will save no one that is wicked and evil.

Yes I know my compassion, but truly let me have no compassion for anyone that is wicked and evil. Lovey, I am so hurt tonight that I want to say I truly don't care anymore but I have to care. I truly love you and I have to be fair and just.

I cannot save a land that is wicked.

Lovey, how did this land, America, the United States of America become so vile and wicked?

When did evil consume this land and people?

I know I have family there but Lovey, can they be saved? Can they be truly saved considering what death and or sin said about them?

Lovey I truly don't know because the hurt and pain is back when it comes to the things we as humans do.

How can anyone say they are a Christian... you know what, I am so not going to go there. I know the wicked and evil as well as the greedy of this world cares not for life. Hence they do not respect your law and laws.

We say "THOU SHALT NOT KILL," but yet we kill anyway. Governments globally send their people on the battlefield to kill hence violating your law. Thus sinning and showing you that they have no respect for you and your laws; word.

So Lovey because of this, no government official that do this, send their people on the battlefield to fight wars that do not concern them, none of their names must be found in your good and true book of life.

They must face their condemnation because they did kill; willingly and knowingly send their citizens out there to take the life of another human being.

Like I said, no one can keep the peace if no peace is within them. Hence no government globally is peaceful. They kill and violate life on a whole period. And none can say I am lying because all I have to do is point at the armies globally, and the funds they allocate to Aries for death and or to take lives.

Yes Lovey I am short tempered but I am coming to you with all and leaving all at your doorstep, no, I am leaving all in your capable hands.

I trust you to do the right thing because I am more than depending on you.

I need true peace here on earth and in the universe Lovey. Hence I am going to tell you again, I want and need no wicked and evil people and spirits in our land and lands. They are more than infinitely and indefinitely locked out more than forever ever without end. Let the devil and or Satan and or Death keep their wicked and evil own.

Psalms One Lovey, hence we (your good and true people who are our good and true people) need you to be with us.

Lovey there is no bargaining anywhere.

Like I said billions did not choose you and I will not step to you and beg for them. I've seen what the wicked can do. Hence remember the 27 years Nelson Mandela spent in jail fighting for the rights of his own people. South Africa is BLACK LAND but yet the blacks of South Africa had no right, all because of the devil's true own. So why would I plead with you for wicked and evil people Lovey?

Why would I sacrifice you for wicked and evil people?

Yes I know not the content of character of the people of PNG, but Lovey what my eyes saw on the internet was not right.

It's just like the musician in Jamaica that got 5 bullets in his head. Hence I've told you that I will not save my Jamaican own because of the wickedness they have done.

We both know that death wants the people of this island hence I've stepped aside from them despite me promoting the island. Death can have them because a beautiful home you gave them including YOUR PRECIOUS AND GORGEOUS NAME, and they the people of Jamaica defiled you.

Instead of keeping your land and name holy, they've done all manner of evil to disrespect and disgrace you. Hence you are no longer with them. Yes they can save self, but like I've told you, I do not trust them to do right by you and for self and this is truly a shame.

Yes I know its Europe's turn, hence the ripe mango you gave to Russia. And like I said; if Russia fails to accept your offer then Europe would have failed.

China is the only one to accept you because they kept the Ying and Yang which is life, and it is also death. The Ying and Yang is a key hence China kept their key.

Africa rejected you due to Ethiopia and there is a hatred in you for Ethiopia. I know this. I know hate is not the proper word, but remember I asked the question using hate and was shown the truth; answer.

Jamaica rejected you and you also deemed the land unclean.

America, the United States of America disgrace and mock you hence they give Aries almost a trillion dollars each year to fight wars; kill. They America claim life, the upward eye in triangle but yet the blood of the innocent is in every American's hand globally. Their military death toll they cannot repay nor can they repay and restore the lives they have taken globally over the years and centuries. Hence when death and or sin talk about sin, they talk about Americans; the citizens of America; the United States of America.

Yes every nation is guilty of this per the dictation of history, but not everyone live to kill another human being for what rightfully belongs to them.

Many have compassion and many are just hence the just and good is saved from what is to come globally.

We cannot say we are all God's children and have no dignity for human life.

We cannot say we are all God's children but have no respect for the next person.

We cannot say we are all God's children but yet give them religions of men; death to condemn and kill them.

We cannot say we are all God's children but yet go behind the next man and or person and rob him her of everything; their heritage, land, resources, lineage, language and god. Come on now. This isn't right. **SO NOW TELL ME, WHEN**

YOU DO ALL THIS, HOW DO YOU EXPECT LOVEY AND OR GOD AND OR GOOD GOD AND ALLELUJAH TO PROTECT AND SAVE YOU?

Do you not stay he has a son that died for you? *BUT INSTEAD OF RESPECTING HIM, YOU MOCKED HIM BY CRUCIFYING HIM ON A CROSS AMONGST A THEIF AND A MURDERER.* **Hence you have no respect for what he has and have done for all of you.**

So tell me, why should Lovey save any of you?

His child you crucified amongst a thief and a murderer and have the nerve to want him Lovey to turn around and save you.

None of you respected him; his child.
None of you shed a tear for him because when he needed water to drink. Water that could have saved him, you gave him bitter gaul mixed with vinegar to drink this according to Matthew in your book of sin; lies and deceit.

Water is the staff of Life people and if he Jesus was Lovey's son then water could have saved him. Let's put it this way, Lovey's water is special blessed. When you ask him to bless you, he rains down water on you. Hence water is abundant in his world and here on earth.

The spirit needs water and without water the spirit cannot live.

But I see ghost.

Please don't go there.
Think final judgment when all that is wicked and evil must come to an end.

But I want it all to end right now you are saying.

So do I, but physical time have to catch up to that point in time. Remember I told you if you've read any of my other books that spiritual time is further ahead in time and physical time must catch up to that point in time.

Hence spiritual time is more advanced.

Wow better stop now.

It's funny because I thought this was going to be my final book, but I have many more to go and yes I've started to write romance again. If I ever complete this story yeah me.

Yes I am cuddled to Lovey because I feel better now. I vented to him in a very crass and abrasive way and I am truly glad I did. Man do I need Fred Hammond right now. Listening to Total Praise and calming my spirit.

So Lovey once again, if I have done wrong in my anger and asking please truly forgive me.

I do not want and need to bring you shame and embarrassment. Lovey, please for my sake, truly let all that is wicked and evil go.

As humans we lie to you and disrespect you.

We kill each other and take what do not belong to us and you cannot continue to let this happen. How would you like it if we did this to you? No wait, we do do this to you on a daily basis and for this I am truly sorry.

We say we love you, but hurt you. And if me taking out my anger on you hurts you, please let me know and truly forgive me because it's not intentional.

And yes I know why I am having severe back pains hence the demons that are around me have to go. My life and lifeline is fragile Lovey. I never knew it was that fragile, hence I have go back to watching clean shows and stop with the demonic and devilish cartoons on Netflix.

Michelle
June 16 – 18, 2015

So as I come to an official close to this book, truly thank you for hearing me out.

Thank you for being there for me. I know you will do the right thing not in anger like me, hence you are my true and good need.

Also thank you for not letting me leave you and whatever you do, never let me leave you. I know I keep telling you I want to go and you keep showing me my end.

Thank you for showing me just how fragile my lifeline is when it comes to the demon spirits of this world.

They do influence hence many walk in the darkness of sin and not in the light of your goodness.

Thank you for showing me the light on your highway because I needed to know and see this, hence the cover of this book.

Michelle

PS. If I've forgotten anything truly forgive me.
And for those who are going to want to send me a
picture of the coconut grove and or plantation in
Portland, Jamaica truly please don't. I am not
allowed to have this picture because Jamaica is
truly not clean and I cannot disobey my spirit nor
can I disobey Lovey. It is not his will for me to
have this picture hence I have to tell you.

Yes Jamaica is beautiful and it's a shame I cannot go home or bask in the beauty of this land anymore. Yes the spirit is hurt and I have to live in the hurt of it.

Yes I took my frustrations out on what's happening in PNG and for some I should not interfere, but I cannot see injustice happen. People, I know what it's like to be robbed of what's rightfully yours because it has happened to me. I will not fight for land, but I will fight for injustice when it comes to my black own. I am sick and tired of people raping the black race and taking their wealth and land from them.

I am sick and tired of other races including my own, massacring the black race like we mean nothing on this earth.

Lovey gave us an abundance of everything and every nation including our own has and have raped us of everything and I am sick and tired of it. You don't kill someone and steal what rightfully belongs to them. You don't want it for you nor would you like it if someone did the same to you, so why the bleep should we as black people (based on hue) like it for us. And Babylonians (based on hue; dark and or black skin) are excluded from this because they did rape us of our god and gave us their dirty and stinking false gods that keep up impoverished and condemned.

Like I said, you can hate me for the words in these books, but the truth is there and the truth can never hurt.

We want to live as the dead without thinking of the consequences. WELL I AM BLEEPING TIRED OF EVERYONE USING THE BLACK RACE. YOU WANT A WAY IN TO LOVEY'S WORLD AND INSTEAD OF GETTING THERE ON YOUR OWN, YOU SACRIFICE THE BLACK RACE BY MASSACRING US AND TAKING WHAT IS RIGHTFULLY OURS. WHILST DOING THIS, YOU MOCK US AND MOCK LIFE INCLUDING THE TRUE AND LIVING GOD OF LIFE. SO BECAUSE OF THIS, I REFUSE ALL WICKED AND EVIL PEOPLE INCLUDING SPIRIT IN THE PHYSICAL AND SPIRITUAL INCLUDING THE UNIVERSE AND HERE ON EARTH.

The black race is no one's scapegoat. <u>YOU BLEEPING HATE US then don't expect us to save you because anyone that is true to their black heritage, language and culture will never save anyone that is wicked and evil.</u> I've made the conscious choice to stand with Lovey in truth, goodness, cleanliness and unison no matter how I battle him for justice and go head to head with him. Do not take what rightfully belongs to another person and say it is yours when you knowingly know it is not yours, come on now man be just and fair.

Lovey don't steal from any of you nor does he steal from his people, so why are you stealing from us and Good God including self?

No man, fair is fair. What you think because you can massacre the black race at WILL MEANS YOU ARE NOT GOING TO BE PUNISHED?

WHY DO YOU THINK THERE'S A HELL?

Listen to Bob Marley's TIME WILL TELL and hear what he said about your thought. Many of you think you are living in heaven but in truth you're living in hell because hell has you locked infinitely and indefinitely, and it's only a matter of time before you get there.

Therefore we were told about heaven and hell, yes the two (2) H's. (Helium)

Hence helium-4 which is the square thus the 3 daughters of Eve (Evening) and their father Satan. Add 3+1=4, the timeline of death and or the time to die which is 24, hence the 24000 Death and or Satan had to take as many of you to hell as he possibly can. Hence billions of you are hell bound literally.

I also forgot, in the My Book Series book 9 or 10 I talked about the two princes. I forgot to add that in the dream Maria told us to sand the edges of the glass down.

And in the dream with the poodle above, the fluffy part of the jet black horse's hind leg or back leg was pinkish white.

Also listen to NATURAL MYSTIC by Bob Marley because he did tell us, "many more would have to suffer," and he is so correct because the massacring of the black race still continues; won't stop. And as time reveals, billions will have hell to pay shortly because the time of the wicked and evil will have come to an end.

Lovey will claim his earth and clean it up for his people and his people alone. As humans we know the truth but yet do not put a conscious effort to and or in stopping the wrongs we are doing. We've made earth a living hell for self and others.

We've made earth a living grave sight of death with our wickedness, but yet expect Lovey to swoop down and clean all up like he's some sort of maid.

Lovey will not do this anymore because he's helped us time and time and again and instead of keeping clean we committed even viler acts of sin.

Now we have the nerve to say he sent his only son to pay the price for us; our sins.

If Lovey kicked Eve the hell out of his domain and she's rotting in hell right now, what make any of you including me special?

Well I am special to him because he's doing all to keep me grounded and safe with him.

We do not choose life and yes life is hard for me but I know why. Hell and the agents of death including some of you in society must make my life a living nightmare for me to fail.

Eve failed because the devil invaded her space and got to her. She did lay with him and procreated.

I refuse death no matter how beautiful and handsome the Devil and or Satan is. I am not interested in the Devil and or Satan because he's not gorgeous enough for me. He's not natural nor is he natural beauty to me. So no, I truly don't want and need him. Good, clean, positive and true life is my choice; hence Lovey is my right and choice. And I refuse to let anyone take him from me.

Life; good and true life is my choice hence he's doing all for me not to fail. But it does not mean the devil isn't trying. Trust me he's trying and trying hard.

Yes Lovey is there but I wish he was more into my life where I am concerned. I truly need him hence when my days are troubled and bad, I will continue to go to him with my aggression, anger, true love and all that ails me.

Writing is my venting and good tool and that good tool and writing is Lovey. Today is bad, but tomorrow is another day and I am good again.

Michelle

OTHER BOOKS BY MICHELLE JEAN

Blackman Redemption – The Fall of Michelle Jean
Blackman Redemption – After the Fall Apology
Blackman Redemption – World Cry – Christine Lewis
Blackman Redemption
Blackman Redemption – The Rise and Fall of Jamaica
Blackman Redemption – The War of Israel
Blackman Redemption – The Way I Speak to God
Blackman Redemption – A Little Talk With Man
Blackman Redemption – The Den of Thieves
Blackman Redemption – The Death of Jamaica
Blackman Redemption – Happy Mother's Day
Blackman Redemption – The Death of Faith
Blackman Redemption – The War of Religion
Blackman Redemption – The Death of Russia
Blackman Redemption – The Truth
Blackman Redemption – Spiritual War
Blackman Redemption – The Youths
Blackman Redemption – Black Man Where Is Your God?

The New Book of Life
The New Book of Life – A Cry For The Children
The New Book of Life – Judgement
The New Book of Life – Love Bound
The New Book of Life – Me
The New Book of Life – Life

Just One of Those Days
Book Two – Just One of Those Days
Just One of Those Days – Book Three The Way I Feel
Just One of Those Days – Book Four

The Days I Am Weak
Crazy Thoughts – My Book of Sin
Broken
Ode to Mr. Dean Fraser

A Little Little Talk
A Little Little Talk – Book Two

Prayers
My Collective
A Little Talk/A Time For Fun and Play
Simple Poems
Behind The Scars
Songs of Praise And Love

Love Bound
Love Bound – Book Two

Dedication Unto My Kids
More Talk
Saving America From A Woman's Perspective
My Collective the Other Side of Me
My Collective the Dark Side of Me
A Blessed Day
Lose To Win
My Doubtful Days – Book One

My Little Talk With God
My Little Talk With God – Book Two

A Different Mood and World – Thinking

My Nagging Day

My Nagging Day – Book Two
Friday September 13, 2013
My True Love
It Would Be You
My Day

A Little Advice – Talk
1313, 2032, 2132 – The End of Man
Tata

MICHELLE'S BOOK BLOG – BOOKS 1 – 20

My Problem Day
A Better Way
Stay – Adultery and the Weight of Sin – Cleanliness
Message

Let's Talk
Lonely Days – Foundation
A Little Talk With Jamaica – As Long As I Live
Instructions For Death
My Lonely Thoughts
My Lonely Thoughts – Book Two
My Morning Talks – Prayers With God
What A Mess
My Little Book
A Little Word With You
My First Trip of 2015
Black Mother – Mama Africa
Islamic Thought
My California Trip January 2015
My True Devotion by Michelle – Michelle Jean
My Many Questions To God

My Talk
My Talk Book Two
My Talk Book Three – The Rise of Michelle Jean
My Talk Book Four
My Talk Book Five
My Talk Book Six
My Talk Book Seven
My Talk Book Eight – My Depression
My Talk Book Nine – Death
My Talk Book Ten - Wow

144pages, June 19, 2015